Waking Up before We Die

Aging and Spirituality

by

Marcelline Hutton

Zea Books
Lincoln, Nebraska
2024

Copyright © 2024 Marcelline Hutton
All rights reserved

ISBN 978-1-60962-334-0 paperback

ISBN 978-1-60962-335-7 ebook

doi 10.32873/unl.dc.zea.1507

Set in Calisto types.

Zea Books are published by the
University of Nebraska–Lincoln Libraries

Electronic (pdf) ebook edition available online at
https://digitalcommons.unl.edu/zeabook/

Print edition available from
https://www.lulu.com/spotlight/unllib

UNL does not discriminate based upon any protected status.
Please go to http://www.unl.edu/equity/notice-nondiscrimination

Dedicated to the spirit that moves us in writing and life

Contents

	Introduction 7
I	Waking Up before We Die 9
II	Waking Up to My Own Aging and Mortality . . 21
III	Musings on Death. 37
IV	Comfort in Death: Funerals. 56
V	Significant Others during Aging and COVID. . . 74
VI	Comfort for Our Heart in Literature 88
VII	Comfort for Our Heart in Music 102
VIII	Other Comforts 105
IX	Upheaval of Moving 116
	Conclusion 143
	Acknowledgments 148

Introduction

And so we do not lose heart.
Tho' the body is wasting away,
The spirit is being renewed day by day.
                                2 Corinthians 4:16

I have heard this scripture from time to time but only recently has it etched itself into my heart and mind. At eighty-four, I realize I am aging, as my body encounters more difficulties. While this is discouraging, the 2 Corinthians 4:16 scripture offers consolation that our spirit is being renewed. In retirement, I have more time for prayer and reflection, to rest in the Lord, and hence to have my spirit renewed. We choose how we interpret our situations. Positive, spiritual aging ideas enhance our sense of well-being. Of course, the loss of loved ones decreases our sense of self-worth at times, but the Spirit can renew us. As Genesis reminds us, God was still working in the lives of Sarah and Abraham in old age, and they can serve as models for us. Indeed, Sarah laughed at the angels and shows us how humor exists even as we age. God wants us to be fully alive at all ages, even old age. While the old nursery rhyme/prayer says

Now I lay me down to sleep
I pray the Lord my soul to keep.
If I should die before I wake,
I pray the Lord my soul to take.

We can also say

If I should wake before I die.

That's our hope, to wake and live before we die.

Chapter I

Waking Up before We Die

Different messengers wake us up, but one of the best is a recent English film called *Living*. It depicts a 1950s buttoned-up London bureaucrat who is diagnosed with terminal cancer and given six months to live. He realizes he'd become a sort of zombie, a half-living and half-dead creature, and he'd like to live a little before he dies. So he does—quite poignantly. The film can be a metaphor for us. We too can wake up before we die and get into the flow of life. The path is unique for each of us. But as we age, we have more time to reflect on how we might want to be more alive, physically, spiritually, and socially. It may start by breathing more deeply. It may start by being quiet, listening, even watching the snow fall. Or by attending a healing service. Whatever occasions "awe" can be a beginning. Sitting by a favorite oak tree, watching the squirrels scamper about the garden. Whatever speaks to us. It may be reading the Scriptures or a novel, listening to music, or going to an art exhibit or the mountains or the seashore. It's tuning in, being aware, and letting our vitality flourish.

Musings on Age and Aging

The other day, my best friend Elaine Kruse celebrated her eighty-third birthday. I reflected on knowing her for forty years and how much her friendship and hospitality have meant to me. I also thought of my lifelong relationship with my sister for over eighty years and that with my cousin Jean for almost eighty years too. Then I thought of my son, sixty years old, and what a wonderful loving relationship that has been with him. I pondered why neither my friend nor I usually think of ourselves as old. Then I remembered the words of my gynecologist in El Paso in the 1990s saying, "We have several ages: our chronological age, our biological age, and our psychological age. They are not always the same." I would add our social and spiritual ages as well. That was the first time I heard that we have several ages. I knew that people often thought I was younger than I was, and I usually hastened to inform them of my chronological age. Now, I see it doesn't really matter.

This morning when I asked my friend Michael Johnson at Pioneer House how he thought about age and why we don't think of ourselves as old, what he said surprised me. He said he thought we have a mental construct of how old we are, and it's not the same as our chronological age. He said he's not old in his mind, and he's always fairly young in his dreams. I had read that we are never old in our dreams. When I asked him about how we square our chronological age with our mental construct, he said that he thought we deceive ourselves, except when we look at pictures of ourselves and see that we sometimes look as old as our chronological age. He added that this self-deception was not a bad thing. A recent article in the *Atlantic* also suggested that people often perceive themselves 20 percent younger than they are. (See Jennifer Senior, "The Age in Your Head," *The Atlantic*, April 2023, pp. 14–16.)

I didn't quite know how to reply to Michael's thoughts. He also suggested we confront our aging when we are sick or feel vulnerable. We don't deceive ourselves then. But, most of the time we don't feel like we are dying, so we fall back into our mental construct of feeling younger. Indeed, an article in the *Wall Street Journal*, "Can Feeling Younger Make You Healthier?" indicated that feeling younger and expecting to grow and develop in later life can add years to our lives. At one point, the article asks us how old we feel regarding our physical abilities, mental performance, and social connections. The answers might not all be the same. (See Betsy Morris, "Can Feeling Younger Make You Healthier?" *Wall Street Journal*, December 6, 2022, p. A16.)

One challenge is that we have never before been old. It's a new experience. Sometimes it's scary, sometimes painful, sometimes overwhelming and depressing. Sometimes we mourn our lost youth and selves. Sometimes we hardly notice because we're absorbed in the present. Although many of my friends and I have been blessed with good health into our seventies, we are aware in our eighties that our faculties have fallen short of what they once were. We still enjoy life but ponder the future and how life is unfolding for us.

Part of our dilemma is that aging is a new season in our lives. We've never been this age before, nor dealt with the physical decline that happens. As far as I can tell, aging is a process. It's not just about retirement and finding new activities. It also involves loss, loss of our old energetic, strong physical selves, and how we cope with these losses. It also involves grief over the loss of loved ones: a spouse, a sibling, a friend. We can lose these significant others in youth or middle age, but it may be harder to cope in old age. I lost my father when I was not yet thirty, but it was not overwhelming. I also lost my husband to divorce when I was thirty-nine, and that was destabilizing. I had to work out a new theology, find new friends, create a new life, and become a new person. Quite a struggle. But I was only thirty-nine years old and weathered the struggle. Losing my mother, this same former husband, and several other relatives and friends in my fifties was mystifying, but I was still working, so I wasn't overwhelmed. Losing my brother in my early eighties was jarring. It saddened me and made me confront my own mortality in ways no other deaths had done. His death plus some health issues opened a new spiritual journey for me. So my increasing physical frailty and loss of family while aging provoked new spiritual awareness of my vulnerability and neediness.

Our spiritual life can help us in dealing with our vulnerability and neediness at any age but especially as we age. By spirituality, I mean in part Christianity with all its rites, rituals, prayers, and Scriptures linking us to the transcendent. I realize this definition doesn't fit everyone. Some people associate spirituality with Jewish, Muslim, or Buddhist rites and rituals. Some think of a "Higher Power," the spirit that moves us, a "reverence for the divine," Transcendental Meditation, or seeking our heart's comfort. Many link spirituality with Nature, finding comfort and healing in Nature with a capital N. This may be the same spirit that we find in art, music, friends, or other sources. None of these views is mutually exclusive. I appreciate Kathleen Fischer's idea in her book *Winter Grace: Spirituality and Aging* that living long we know something about the brokenness of life as well as its blessings. She shows how we can nourish others with our brokenness and blessings (p. 20). She sees Jesus bringing dejected people energy for newness of life. Spirituality to her is not just for the old but all ages (pp. 11 and 16). As Fischer reminds us, God's word helps us move with confidence and hope (p. 17). Indeed, Fischer's book is one of the best I have read on the subject of aging and spirituality. Three other good books are psychologist Connie Zweig's *The Inner Work of Age: Shifting from Role to Soul*, psychologist Becca Levy's *Breaking the Age Code*, and sociologist Morrie Schwartz's *The Wisdom of Morrie: Living and Aging Creatively and Joyfully*. All are challenging and helpful for adopting more positive attitudes toward aging. A friend in Iowa City, Laura Julier, suggested several of these books to me in the summer of 2022 when I saw her at lunch one day. She had trained as a hospital chaplain in Michigan before her retirement, and she had read them. I am indebted to all of them but found Fischer's and Schwartz's books the most congenial. All remind us that inner growth and full lives are possible for us as we age. But Fischer and Schwartz deal more with our spiritual journey and affirm life in the face of death (Fischer, p. 11).

Dr. David Lipschitz notes in his book *Breaking the Rules of Aging* that spirituality for many involves less formal beliefs than organized religion. For many it embraces a sense of community and oneness with the world and the people around them. As a physician he took his patients' spiritual leanings seriously. He remarks: "people who cultivate their spiritual sides tend to be healthier than those who don't." (See David A. Lipschitz, *Breaking the Rules of Aging*, Washington, DC: Lifeline Press, 2002, p. 248.) He cites studies that link people who are religious to healthier and longer lives. He wasn't sure what it is about religious or spiritual beliefs that promote good health, only that prayer, meditation, and worship embrace the positive emotions of hope and love. People involved in religious communities tend to spend time with like-minded people who give them a sense of connectedness and belonging, qualities linked to longevity. He doesn't claim to know how spirituality and prayer affect health, only that they're beneficial (p. 249). Likewise, therapist Becca Levy in her book *Breaking the Age Code* indicates that our beliefs affect our longevity. Using evidence from an age study of the residents of one Ohio town, she found that positive age beliefs lengthen our lives 7.5 years. Likewise, negative age beliefs and denigration of the aged shorten the life span of people. (See Levy, *Breaking the Age Code*, p. 93.) Jimmy Carter in his book *The Virtues of Aging* asserts similar arguments, and Morrie Schwartz also warns against adopting negative ageist attitudes. In later chapters I discuss religious, literary, musical, and other comforts that come our way as we age.

My essay is not so much about developing spirituality in order to live longer and healthier but more about the solace we find that makes life worth living. It's about the comfort available to us amidst our afflictions and fears of death. As a verse in Isaiah says, God will wipe away every tear (Isaiah 25:8). Whether we cry from physical or emotional aches and pains, it's good to know the Spirit comforts us. As the body slows down because of chronic illness or is wracked with disease and pain, the life of the spirit can revive us in the midst of our suffering. Indeed, we may be revived to enjoy new encounters as they occur. By spirituality I mean experiences of inner knowing of the Holy that can emerge from practices like meditation, prayer, and activities we can engage in daily, not just in weekly church, synagogue, temple, or mosque services. Our inner knowing becomes part of our creative response to life and finding purpose in our lives. As Kathleen Fischer points out in *Winter Grace*, old age is a unique spiritual journey for each of us. It can reveal the mystery of life to us. We learn that our self-worth is not determined by consumerism or possessions (Fischer, *Winter Grace*, pp. 13–15).

Attending a gospel piano concert the other evening at Eastmont, the retirement community I moved to in June 2024, I was reminded of how African American spirituals have influenced American spirituality. As a result, I've been singing "Nobody knows the trouble I've seen / Nobody knows but Jesus," which is very comforting. Several years ago, I remember looking up the lyrics to "There Is a Balm in Gilead"—"There is a balm in Gilead / to heal the sin-sick soul"—and this too was comforting to sing. Thinking of other spirituals, such as "He's Got the Whole World in His Hands," "Every Time I Feel the Spirit" (Ev'ry time I feel the Spirit / moving in my heart, I will pray)," or "Swing Low, Sweet Chariot," I connect with the Spirit. I'm sort of healing myself with song. When we feel mournful, it's good to sing one of these spirituals and be lifted up. As Corinthians tells us, the Spirit renews us. And it can renew us in song as well as other ways. Or the songs can remind us that others, including American slaves, have had it hard but persevered with God's help. The song reminds us we can too. (The lyrics are available by Google search, if you feel like singing.) Romans 8:26–27 tells us that when we don't have words, the Spirit intercedes for us with wordless sighs. Our sighs and groanings can be prayer.

Morrie Schwartz suggests that we use our imagination to develop our own image of a supreme being or of the power of the universe. We can use our imagination to attain spiritual enlightenment. (See Morrie Schwartz, *The Wisdom of Aging*, edited by Rob Schwartz, Philadelphia: Blackstone, p. 36.) In retirement we have time to let our imagination roam. As a meditator, he's also concerned with mindfulness and awareness. One of Schwartz's greatest insights is seeing how we learn to balance our feelings and moods, which swing from hope to despair, with feelings of vitality falling into tiredness and depression. We have contradictory feelings that life is worth living versus all the good has already happened and the future is bleak (pp. 74–75). He then asserts that as we become more aware of our emotional needs and moods, we can observe them, gain some control over them, and accommodate to our new situation (pp. 76–82).

By the term "aging," I do not mean decrepitude. I first heard this word used by a friend I met on a cruise several years ago. He was a fellow academic, and I liked him a lot. But I took umbrage against his frequently expressed fear of decrepitude. Aging can be a natural process that happens and that we adjust to. Decrepitude implies a stigma, loathsomeness, and disability that I don't think my friends and I feel, at least not so much right now. As Schwartz indicates, the body may be decaying, but the mind and spirit may remain intact (p. 141). However, as my body deteriorates, I have begun to revise my ideas and realize how much more effort everything takes. It also dawned on me that the fellow on the cruise was caring for his wife who had multiple sclerosis. That is a debilitating disease. So, perhaps it was his wife's decline that made him speak of decrepitude.

Aging Well

Jimmy Carter's book *The Virtues of Aging* remains timely, although it was written twenty-five years ago. His major arguments are that we need to exercise daily and devote ourselves to some sort of useful work. After losing his reelection bid at fifty-six years of age, he and Rosalynn both wrote books and volunteered for many organizations, including Habitat for Humanity. Carter knew what it meant to lose his job in the prime of life. Reagan had defeated him, and he experienced involuntary retirement (Carter, *The Virtues of Aging*, New York: Ballentine, 1998, pp. 1–3). Yet he did not sit around moaning and groaning, as many would have done, but swung into action writing his memoir of the presidency, as a publisher urged him to do. He and Rosalynn returned to their home and family in Plains, Georgia, and established a healthy routine of exercise, work, and time with friends and family. They jogged, rode their bikes, and fished together. They even learned to ski in middle age. Later they hiked in the mountains in Nepal and climbed Mount Kilimanjaro. He thought exercising aided the lungs and bones as well as our mental health. (Modern research supports this. Indeed, a book review in the March 30, 2023, *Wall Street Journal*, p. A15, suggests that vigorous exercise can extend life ten years over a sedentary existence. Moreover, exercise-based interventions have been more effective than some pharmaceuticals in reducing mortality from heart disease, diabetes, and stroke. See Matthew Rees, "Heaven Can Wait," a review of Peter Attia and Bill Gifford's *Outlive: The Science and Art of Longevity*, *Wall Street Journal*, March 30, 2023, p. 15). Carter also thought exercise along with a healthy diet helped lower blood pressure, cholesterol, body fat, and blood sugar (pp. 3–4, 55–57). Ideas like his are being proven decades later. Having an active lifestyle was a key to their happy life. Jimmy also did woodworking, making chairs, tables, and beds for a log cabin they built near a Georgia river. Jimmy and Rosalynn were unusual in that they divided the chores of running their farm business between them and brought it back from the $1 million in debt that they had encountered when they first retired (pp. 37–39).

Carter's prescriptions for good health besides exercise included a healthy diet and avoiding smoking and drinking. He also endorsed strong social ties with family and friends and a purpose in work and or volunteering (pp. 56–57). These points are espoused by many others today. Some of the virtues that he identified included wisdom, which he defined as good judgment in uncertain times (p. 13). (Others also attribute wisdom to age but don't define it so clearly.) He admitted that having grown up on a farm during the Depression had made him financially frugal and cautious. Another virtue he identified involved facing death with faith and courage, not fear, anguish, or distress (p. 62). In his nineties, he is doing just that, having given himself up to hospice and asking that no extraordinary measures be taken for prolonging his life. Engaging with life is another virtue he touted. By this he meant interacting with friends and carrying out productive activities, which for him and Rosalynn included writing more books, since their first were so successful. He concluded his book with a reference to St. Paul's celebration of love in 1 Corinthians about faith, hope, and love as well as the epigram "We are old when regret takes the place of dreams" (p. 134).

The most humorous book I have read about aging is by

Margareta Magnusson, called *The Swedish Art of Aging Exuberantly*. While much of the book is taken up with anecdotes about raising her five children in Sweden, the United States, and Singapore, she intersperses some helpful nuggets about aging. One I had never thought of is making your routines dear to you (p. 116). Schwartz also emphasizes the importance of routine in exercise, meditation, and time with friends. Magnusson also urged people to go with the flow instead of getting angry (p. 104). Her third admonition is to downsize your abode and rid it of all superfluous objects. The Swedish call this "death cleaning," getting rid of things so your children won't have to. She tells of one friend who recycles books, makeup, and even food whenever she brings something new home (pp. 35 and 131–141). A fourth is about noticing wrinkles after cataract surgery. Apparently the author was shocked at all the wrinkles she saw after surgery improved her vision. At first she was dismayed. Then she realized that all her friends had already seen her with all these wrinkles, and they still loved her. They were new only to her, and she didn't have to be so upset about them (pp. 66–68). Fifth, she nearly died from heart failure, and she was hardly conscious of the whole incident. After surgery, she recovered, and this taught her not to fear death. It didn't hurt. Her lesson is taking everything in stride (pp. 39–46). Sixth, take care of your hair, if you have some (pp. 67–70). Other ideas are fairly common: phone friends while enjoying a gin and tonic; volunteer; enjoy young children; and eat chocolate (Margareta Magnusson, *The Swedish Art of Aging Exuberantly*, New York: Scribner, 2022).

While many of these authors wrote out of a desire to help others age well, I must confess that I began writing this treatise from the terror I felt prior to an operation in April 2021.

I resisted the surgeries on my prolapsed uterus and bladder as long as I could, but when the pain became too great, I was motivated to have the operations. After the successful surgeries, I realized that my fear of the operations was masking a fear of death. So I decided to explore the issues of aging, death, and spirituality. Why was I so afraid of dying? A friend and I reassured each other periodically that we have lived long, rich lives and need not fear death. So, why was I so scared? Human, all too human, I decided.

As I reflected on these concerns about death and dying, it occurred to me that maybe these issues bothered others as well. I asked some friends at church if they'd be interested in discussing these ideas in our adult forum. Several said "yes." Next, I checked with our priest to make sure such a discussion was OK with him. It was. So, I called a retired priest, Mary Hendricks, who suggested something we might use for our discussions. She recommended *Soul Unfinished* by British bishop Robert Atwell. It's a good book but seemed more about retirement than aging and spirituality. So dissatisfaction with his book was another impetus to write my own.

Chapter II

Waking Up to My Own Aging and Mortality

While my surgeries in April 2021 were a wakeup call, in all honesty, I have to admit that my diagnosis with the chronic disease bronchiectasis in 2009–10 was what first nudged me into thinking sotto voce about aging and mortality. Until that time, I had been remarkably healthy and needed no prescriptions. Having been a walker all my life, and having low blood pressure, I thought of myself as a normal, healthy person. Indeed, I seldom thought of health or death. I just walked where and when I wanted. I went on holidays when I could afford them and enjoyed life researching and writing books on Russian women's history as well as two memoirs during retirement in my seventies. This pattern continued until my eighties. Then, it became harder to walk very far without stopping to catch my breath. In the fall of 2021, I was diagnosed with mycobacterium avium complex (MAC) for the third time. And my pulmonologist told me I'd have to take antibiotics for the rest of my life. A stern warning, and a bit of a downer. I had considered illness and aging a bit bothersome but not divine messengers, as Connie Zweig does in her book *The Inner Work of Age: Shifting from Role to Soul*. In retrospect, I can now view them as catching my attention and see them as divine warnings for preparation for death.

While declining health wakes up many of us to aging, our awareness comes in different ways. A dear, and very healthy, friend confided in me that she had never considered herself old until she had a great-grandchild. It was then that she realized she probably wouldn't live to see him grow up to be an adult. She enjoys remarkably good health and exercises regularly, so that may be why she hadn't thought about aging, even though she's in her late seventies. One of my aunts had never thought of herself as old until she heard a TV commentator describe a ninety-year-old as elderly. It surprised me that this aunt had never considered herself old until she heard someone label her so. Maybe that's why she lived to be ninety-four in reasonably good health. I guess the people who surprise me most are those I consider middle-aged who worry about aging. I certainly never thought about aging when I was in my forties, fifties, or sixties. But we are all unique. Also, I was just beginning my teaching career at forty, whereas many had been working for some time by then.

Indeed, my brother's death in July 2020 in Tucson, Arizona, at the age of eighty-three sent me into a funk that I had a hard time getting out of. After his death, I lolled on my chaise longue watching movies on the Turner Classic Movies channel and reading novels and mysteries from our local library. Nothing wrong with these activities, but I got bogged down in them for more than a year. I had a hard time finishing research on an essay/lecture on British women diarists during World War II and a harder time writing it up. I still haven't typed in all the footnotes. This happened during COVID-19, so maybe that had a bigger impact on me than I have realized. Since I lived in a cooperative apartment in Pioneer House in Lincoln, Nebraska, and could meet and talk with friends in the lobby as well as take a trolley bus downtown to the library, Walgreens, Wendy's, or St. Mark's Episcopal Church, I had assumed I was not feeling the effects of COVID. But maybe I was.

What I do know is that God can speak to us through illness. Our afflictions may nudge us into finding greater inner resources and a deeper spirituality. The recent death of my friend Beth Hemmer at Pioneer House in January 2022 also served as a motivator to start writing about aging, death, and spirituality.

Death as a Motivator

While I had been wanting to write on aging and spirituality for several months, it was still a surprise one Tuesday morning in the midst of doing my laundry that I sat down and began writing while waiting for my clothes to dry. In retrospect, I wondered if death sometimes serves as a motivator as well as a depressant. When my brother died, I felt depressed for months. Before his death, I seldom turned on the TV until 6:00 to watch the PBS evening news. Then I would often watch a movie from 7:00 till 9:00. After Walt's death, however, I found myself watching the 3:00 and sometimes even the 1:00 movie. When I told my priest about my lassitude, he suggested two antidotes: (1) read a Psalm every day, and (2) volunteer to do something for someone else. I found an old edition of the Psalms called *Psalms Now* by Leslie Brandt and fell in love with it. The Psalms had always been one of my favorite books of the Bible, and Brandt's adaptation of Psalm 95 is uplifting to read:

Waking Up before We Die

Let us begin this day with singing,
Whether we feel like it or not,
Let us make glad sounds
And force our tongues to articulate words
Of thanksgiving and praise.

The facts are: God is with us;
This world and we who live in it are His.
He loves us;
He has adopted us as His children;
We belong to Him.
This makes us valid, worthwhile.
We are truly significant in the eyes of our God
Irrespective of our human feelings
Or the comments of our critics about us.

This may not be the way we feel this morning,
But this is the way it is.
We don't need the plaudits of our peers,
For we have God's stamp of approval.

So let us begin this day with singing
Whether we feel like it or not.
Then we may end this day with praises,
Because we know—and may even feel
That we shall forever be
The objects of God's concern
And the children of His love.

This adaptation was written before inclusive language became common, but if we overlook the androcentric words, it's very comforting. How I wish I had known the idea about being a child of God earlier in my life. Had I known this, I wouldn't have spent so much time and energy trying to get my husband to love me. I would have known God loved me, and that was enough. Indeed, it took a divorce to show me that my husband didn't love himself very much, so why did I expect him to love me? It took even longer for me to realize that I didn't love myself very much, so why did I expect someone else to love me? As I recovered from divorce, I began to realize I needed a new theology since the old judgmental, patriarchal ideas from my childhood no longer worked. Fortunately for me, this was the time of feminist theology and new ways of imagining God as creator, redeemer, sustainer. I began to hear: "We are all icons, made in the image of God" and "You are a child of God and God loves you." How hopeful and helpful these words and ideas were. I also remember our priest Anne Baker in Iowa City in the 1980s preaching on a sermon from Isaiah: "A bruised reed God would not crush, nor a flickering light extinguish." It felt good hearing those words. God wasn't only the punishing, avenging God of my childhood but a gentle, caring God, as our shepherd.

As I age, I am more able to embrace this loving, nurturing God. I know God doesn't abandon us in old age but continues to minister to us through the Holy Spirit, scripture, friends, and Nature—old oak trees outside my windows, sunshine, snow, even cloudy days. Indeed, when I read a sad email about the death of an old high school chum recently, an antidote arrived the next day in an email from another friend citing the creativity of Pablo Casals, the famous cellist, who at ninety-three was still working. So, once again, the gut-wrenching hurt of death or illness balanced by a life-affirming event; once again the Spirit speaking through a "cloud of witnesses."

Humor

While death can be a downer or a motivator, I've recently encountered humor in my morning devotions. God continues to surprise me. The other day as I was composing a ditty to sing before breakfast, following the advice of Psalm 95, I found myself chuckling at the rhyme I had found for sunshine. For several days I had sung "Thank you for sunshine, it warms up my heart," and then the words that came were, "Thank you for sunshine, it lights up the dark." Or, "Thank you for sunshine, it brightens the skies / Thank you for sunshine, it brightens our lives."

It pleased me that the words rhymed. In the winter in Nebraska, where I live, it can be pretty dark at 8:00 a.m. So having the sun burst out is marvelous. I laugh to myself when a rhyme comes. Sometimes it is hard to find a word that rhymes with sunshine, heart, or gray day, but the singing lifts my mood. On the first day of spring, what came to me was "Thank you for springtime, we really like it. / Thank you for springtime, it sure is a hit." Or, in October, I sang "Thank you for new days, they offer us hope. / Thank you for new days, they widen our scope."

It's harder to praise the bleak, gray days of winter. Yet often a word or a tune comes. The Spirit that moves us provides the wherewithal when I quiet myself. If I listen for a word to be revealed, something happens. That's a delicious experience. Quite different from the automatic lyrics that roll off my tongue when I'm singing about sunshine, but ones worth waiting for. I've reconciled myself to the fact that bleakness is part of winter. It's OK. Feeling comforted by the Holy Spirit about the dreariness of winter is as profound as the uplift of the sunny mornings. This morning's lyrics were "Thank you for snow, Lord, it brightens my day / Thank you for snow, Lord, it lightens my way." During our dreary spring days, I've learned to sing "Thank you for gray days, they bring on the rain / Thank you for gray days, they help the terrain." And "Thank you for dark skies, they cause me to wonder. / Thank you for dark skies, they bring on the thunder." I love the power of the word "thunder." Since our entire state has been in a drought, we're grateful for precipitation.

God's Provision

Maybe accepting the bleak and dreary is part of the mystery of aging. Although the body is slowing down with aches and pains, the message remains that life is worth living. Life still surprises us. If we're willing to be still, we'll be touched. Awe is something we can experience and cultivate at any age. Moreover, we have more time for quiet and awe in retirement. God provides new journeys, endeavors, and experiences. And the Spirit that moves us equips us to undertake them. In our communion service there's a phrase about God providing newness of life (*Book of Common Prayer*, p. 363). In old age we can notice the dialectic movement of the soul's growth and process.

Pondering my diagnosis of bronchiectasis when I turned seventy, I began to see a correlation between illness and God's provision. I was living in a friend's house in Ft. Lauderdale, Florida, in 2009 when I had a panic attack at Christmas. I was alone and feeling alienated. I had retired from teaching at Lithuania Christian College (LCC), where I taught from 2000 to 2008. But settling into American life proved more difficult than expected. I ended up buying a cooperative apartment in Lincoln, Nebraska, because I had two friends teaching there, and it seemed like a good enough place to live. Not wanting to face winter there, I decided to winter in Florida in the unoccupied home of my graduate school friend Janusz Duzinkiewicz. It seemed a dream solution. His house was located in a safe neighborhood close to an Episcopal church and within walking distance of some grocery stores and the Broward County Library. This was an amazing library with a park, a small pool, and palm trees outside the building plus palm trees, newspapers, and good books inside. What more did I need? I was working on a travel memoir at the time, and the library offered computers for me to use free of charge to type my writing. Janusz also lent me his library card, so I could check out books. His house was located just a couple blocks from the main street called Las Olas, which had buses and trolleys that went to the beach.

I was settling in there and working on my book called *Falling in Love with the Baltics*. It had been unnerving learning to write in the first person singular, as one editor had insisted I do. After fifty years of writing history lectures, articles, and a book in the third person—that is, "it seemed," "it appeared," or "it happened"—I found it unsettling to write "I thought," "I traveled," and so forth. Eventually, I adjusted, and life was going OK. I was meeting people at All Saints Episcopal Church on Sunday and at the small Wednesday healing service. Most of the people I met were either full-time Florida residents or permanent snowbirds who owned their own condos and had their own circle of friends.

Everyone I knew was celebrating the holidays with old friends, and I wasn't included. I felt really lonely Christmas day, and I had a panic attack. I'd seen a sign about counselors not far from All Saints Episcopal Church, so the next day I went to check it out and write down the phone number. I thought maybe a therapist could help me. To my dismay, the phone number didn't work, so I felt even more isolated and abandoned. Although my sister insisted that Christmas was just one day, and I'd get through it, somehow, I was lonesome and deeply troubled. While Janusz's house was in an ideal location in many ways, it lacked neighbors. Some of the nearby houses were empty, and other nearby buildings were businesses: a school, a veterinary clinic, and a doctor's office, all closed on holidays. So there weren't any people nearby or neighbors to talk to. Feeling overwhelmed, I later went to a doctor to see if there was any physical reason for my breathing trouble. Dr. Fiorello was kind and compassionate but really into tests. I had blood tests, thyroid tests, and then consulted a pulmonologist, who did even more tests, diagnosing me with bronchiectasis. I'd never heard of this, and it sounded scary. All these tests took two months, and by then I was ready to return to Lincoln. When I came home, I found a pulmonologist through my friend Pat Green at Pioneer House and went to see him. After X-rays, he said he thought a dark place in my lungs indicated cancer. I told him I couldn't possibly have lung cancer because I walked three miles a day and ate three meals a day. How could I have lung cancer? He insisted on a bronchoscopy to take some tissue from my lung to see what the shadow was. The thought of a doctor putting a tube down my throat freaked me out. It took months before I agreed to that. As the daughter of an alcoholic, I had learned to deny reality and had practiced it much of my life. So it took a while to break through my denial and get the needed bronchoscopy. At first I thought, "I don't have to have this procedure. I'm seventy years old and have had a good life. I can just let myself die." Then I thought, "I don't want my son to be orphaned. If I die, he'll be an orphan." (His father was already dead.) Finally, I decided that I didn't want to die but wanted to live and decided it was OK to have the test. It turned out I had an infection called MAC, which could be treated with a combination of three different antibiotics a day for a year. I followed that treatment and recovered from the MAC but not the bronchiectasis, which is a chronic, untreatable disease.

Illness, Transformation, and Compensation

Almost as compensation for my illness, several months later I heard of a course in discernment at nearby St. Paul United Methodist Church in Lincoln. On Wednesday nights the church offered supper and a variety of classes. Since my church, St. Mark's on the Campus, did not offer midweek services or courses, I was eager to join one at St. Paul. Fortunately, one didn't have to be a member there to participate. The course that interested me was taught by Steve Griffith, who had chosen a book by Parker Palmer. What I remember most about the course was the story of Abraham, who at seventy was directed by God to go to a new land and a new life. I realized then that maybe my

Waking Up to My Own Aging and Mortality

life wasn't over at seventy. So, I began thinking about what God had in store for me. One upshot was that I wrote three books in my seventies, and more importantly found two new spiritual resources: St. Luke's Healing Ministry and Camp Farthest Out.

In the summer of 2010, Roger Wait, a parishioner at St. Mark's, invited people to St. Luke's Healing Ministry, which met once a month at St. Matthew's Episcopal Church on Saturday mornings. This was a small group of people who met for prayer, communion, and a healing service in the chapel as well as study about healing in the library. This was just what I needed, given my recent diagnoses. It turned out that Roger drove me to the monthly meetings for about eight years. Being involved with this healing ministry helped me heal spiritually and renew my spirit. I especially appreciated the laying on of hands when people prayed for me, and the hugs we gave each other during the peace before communion. Both were healing and reassuring.

Later at St. Mark's, I heard Mary Roseberry-Brown mention a weeklong summer retreat called Camp Farthest Out, or CFO. It was held at a dormitory at a college in Fremont, Nebraska, and provided time for prayer, singing, and listening to inspiring messages. Soon, this camp became an annual retreat for me, and I realize in retrospect that it too was part of God's provision for me after my MAC diagnosis. Indeed, I met a healer at the camp who suggested I rub an oil-based garlic solution on my chest every night because garlic is antibacterial. This treatment, plus the prayers of those at the camp and my antibiotics, helped cure the disease. Indeed, all the prayers and a healthy lifestyle kept me in good shape until 2018 when the MAC returned. Then I had to take another round of antibiotics for a year. It turns out that bacteria in the air, water, or earth can cause MAC. It was all around me, especially in the air in windy, windy Nebraska. Only long after I moved did I discover that Nebraska is the windiest state in the entire union. In the fall of 2021, Dr. Fiedler, my pulmonologist, indicated that once again the MAC was back. Thus, in the spring of 2022, I waited for an appointment with Dr. Smith, an infectious diseases doctor, who concocted a familiar antibiotic cocktail for me. Since this is my third bout, it isn't so frightening. Unsettling and bothersome, yes; terrifying, no. So, here I am again with low energy trying to write this piece on aging and spirituality yet sustained by the Spirit that moves us.

A comment I heard in our adult forum on aging made me think of John Donne's *Devotions upon Emergent Occasions*. Rereading Devotion 17, "No Man Is an Island," I noticed his very different approach toward illness and death. He viewed affliction as a boon: "… affliction is a treasure, and scarce any may hath enough of it. No man hath affliction enough that is not matured and ripened by it, and made fit for God by that affliction" (Donne, *Devotions upon Emergent Occasions*, originally published in 1624, republished by Ann Arbor Paperbacks, University of Michigan Press, 1960, p. 109). Donne concluded: "… they that find not joys in their sorrows, nor glory in their dejections in this world, are in a fearful danger of missing both in the next" (Donne, p. 111).

In old age I am taking some time to ponder these words. Only now do I see that painful as divorce was, it freed me to become who I am, writing not only my dissertation but publishing five books. Most of all, it freed me to learn to love and accept myself and others.

Writing and typing this book, I find more evidence of God's

provision during aging. I'm not as disciplined as I used to be. When I was in my forties, I wrote or typed in the morning, beginning about 10:00. In my seventies, I began writing at 11:00 or typing at 1:00. Now in my eighties, I intend to do that but often find myself watching a movie on TCM or reading a mystery in the afternoon instead. Sometimes, I write and type in the afternoon between 2:00 and 4:00, or even as late at 7:00 p.m. I seldom work in the morning. My body and spirit aren't ready. Still, I'm grateful for even my weaker discipline. At least the Spirit strengthens and empowers me to write and type a little. I still remember a professor at the University of Iowa who told me that if I worked just one hour a day, I would finish my dissertation. I was shocked. Yet it proved true. If I sat down to work for one hour, I often worked longer. Now, I occasionally work a half hour a day—not a good recipe for finishing my book, but it's working. After reading Morrie Schwartz's book, however, I felt more motivated to write or type. Hooray for Morrie!

At Pioneer House, I sometimes grappled with having no pressing need to get up in the morning. I had few duties, functions, or events to attend to. So after reading one of the two newspapers I subscribe to, I would get up at 7:00, 8:00, or even 9:00. Sometimes I luxuriated in the softness and warmth of my bed after reading the paper and dozed off or let my mind wander. This wasn't all bad. The other day the Spirit moved me to think of a friend who is confined to a wheelchair and is now in a nursing home. This person lived and worked in Ukraine years ago, so I decided to call her to see how she was faring during all the news of the war there. I was glad I did. She was happy to have someone to talk to.

Five years ago, I had more energy and discipline. I just got up and did my morning exercises as though on automatic pilot. Getting up when I woke up was easy. Not so much any more. Our habits can change as we age. It's not wrong to read the paper in bed and doze off; it's just more of an effort to get up and get going. Maybe this is what Mary Pipher meant in her book *Women Rowing North* by our needing to make more effort. I'm not sure. It's hard to know if this change is because of aging, sloth, MAC, or COVID, which discouraged us from going out and about. Indeed, even in early 2023, I felt as if I were engaged in "cautionary living," as a friend put it in her Christmas newsletter. After taking my antibiotics for a few months, however, I was pleased that I could get up more easily, do my exercises, and go for a walk before breakfast. Then I felt refreshed to enter the day's activities. However, this was before the really cold weather hit in January and February 2023 and squashed any desire to go outside, let alone go for a fifteen-minute walk. Not walking in the morning, I easily fell back into slothful habits and lacked stamina. It seems that as we age we are more easily traumatized by our circumstances and the weather. Neither seemed to have such debilitating effects upon us when we were younger. Maybe as we age, we become more fragile and have to put forth more effort to do what we need to do. Or, maybe we decide not to bother with certain activities at all.

What surprised me a lot one very cold Sunday morning was that several older people like me showed up to discuss aging and spirituality in the adult forum at St. Mark's. So, aging doesn't always hold us back if we have something we'd like to do. Indeed, one of the most helpful things I read in Atwell's book *Soul Unfinished* was a quote from a ninety-three-year-old Brit saying: "Take risks." He was tired of people telling him to

"Take care." This was delightful!

Atwell didn't clarify what risks one should take but left it up to us. In the adult forum we didn't come to any conclusions about what risks to take, but I decided it didn't mean physical risks, like going without a mask during COVID, but maybe psychological risks—doing something new. I think I may have one more trip in me, and I'd like to go to southern France. For a long time I've wanted to see Carcassonne, Arles, Avignon, and other cities with Roman ruins. Also, after reading Martin Walker's mysteries about a provincial policeman named Bruno, I've become enthusiastic about seeing provincial France. Although I love traveling to Russia to see St. Petersburg and other areas I've read about as a Russian historian, I adore France as the intriguing "other." Growing up in northern Indiana, I was aware of French-speaking Quebec and longed to see it. Taking two years of French in high school deepened this longing, and I thought all things French chic and alluring. I still do. So, if I have one more trip left in me, I'd love for it to be to France. Rural England has its charms, especially Derbyshire in the spring with the blooming trees and flowers and cavorting lambs in the fields, but it's France that beguiles me. Lately, however, I've begun to think the salty air and sandy beaches of the Portuguese coast might refresh my lungs, knees, and feet more. So, maybe it'll be Portugal and not France where I'll visit. We'll see.

In the adult forum, we also discussed how we felt freer as we age, less concerned with public opinion. I noticed this same idea in Kathleen Fischer's book *Winter Grace*. In chapter 10, she writes that as we age, we feel freer. We are less dependent on others' opinions and more willing to take risks and stand up for what we believe. Indeed, we become winter grace for ourselves and others (pp. 195 and 197).

In our forum, we briefly discussed how transformative illness and distress could be, how it could draw us closer to God. We didn't discuss our maladies in detail, neither their negative nor positive aspects. We didn't dwell long on the transformative possibilities of illness. So, I was quite intrigued when I read a book review about this process in the life of Franklin D. Roosevelt. It was called *Becoming FDR: The Personal Crisis That Made a President* by Jonathan Darman. His contention is that polio changed Roosevelt from a handsome, aristocratic dilettante to a more serious and compassionate man, a man who could become great partly because of his suffering and struggle to walk again. Indeed, the author's quote from Frances Perkins, FDR's later secretary of labor, sums up the situation. Before polio, Perkins thought FDR delightfully charming and talented but vain and insincere. She argues: "I would like to think that he would have done the things he did without his paralysis, but I don't think he would have unless somebody had dealt him a blow between the eyes" (in *Becoming FDR* by Jonathan Darman, New York: Random House, 2022, p. 240). It took polio to "wake up" FDR to greatness. Indeed, as Darman asserts, adversity at any age can make us better, more alive, more aware of others, more useful and successful, more aware of our own potential and possibilities (p. xxvii).

Chapter III

Musings on Death

As I was pondering a friend's death recently, I began to realize that death affects us differently, depending on our relationship to the one who has died. When I was three, my mother took me to view the body of my Great-grandfather Iselman, who had died at age eighty-five. I remember her holding me by the hand in the funeral home as we approached the casket to view Great-grandpa's body. I don't remember any of the words spoken on this occasion, but I do remember the somber nature of the event, the subdued voices of my relatives, and the respect with which we viewed the body and quietly spoke to friends and relatives. In retrospect, I can see that his death did not affect me and perhaps my mother too much. At eighty-five, his death would have been in the natural order of things. Yet it probably caused my Great-grandmother Iselman considerable grief.

When I was twelve, the death of my aunt Margaret had only a marginal impact on me. She and her family lived in the country in a trailer next to my Grandfather and Grandmother Johnson. Since my family did not own a car, we seldom saw my grandparents or this aunt and her family. What I recall from her funeral, at the funeral dinner, is some rather disapproving discussion by some of my relatives about this aunt. I didn't know what to make of it but didn't talk to my mother or sister about it. Speaking to my sister about this death recently, it turned out that it affected her more than me. Hearing our relatives criticize this aunt for "drinking and running around," she noted their disapproval. From this she deduced that they did not treat outsiders kindly and decided that she could not count on them for support. So she chose friends outside our extended family for comfort. I didn't feel this estrangement and kept close to my aunts and their families for decades.

What I didn't realize then was how devastating this event was for my cousins, who had lost their mother. Their lives were changed forever, since they were all less than twelve years old. I knew that my grandmother and maiden aunt who lived next door took care of them, and they became these cousins surrogate parents, since their father was a long-distance truck driver and often away. My mother and other aunts did not mention their plight to me, so I had no idea how difficult it probably was for them. At family reunions in the summer when I saw them, they seemed OK. They ate and played like the rest of us. I never thought of these cousins as bereaved or semi-orphaned because they were part of our extended family, which seemed to shelter them within it. Also, the two youngest were much younger than I, so we seldom played together. Since they lived in the country, we didn't go to the same church or schools, and I seldom saw them. In the 1940s and 1950s when I was growing up, the death of a parent was pretty rare, as was divorce. Families tended to remain intact. So, again, this death did not affect me terribly but rather it did my cousins who had lost their mother.

Looking back, I wondered about compensation occurring after my aunt's death. It was when I was about twelve that my sister and I decided to be baptized and become members of the La Porte Presbyterian Church. This changed our lives as we became more involved in Sunday school and the junior high choir, enjoying church life through singing and the touching sermons of our minister, the Reverend Didier. My sister Kathryn and I walked together to choir practice on Wednesday nights and to church on Sunday mornings. Singing in the choir provided us a sense of belonging. Indeed, our choir director was so gifted in working with young people that she included a young man who played cello along with the majestic organ. I remember how much it meant to learn Haydn's oratorio *The Creation* and how exciting it was to have a choir concert at the church and then later go on a tour of churches in the Detroit area. We even got to go to Windsor, Canada. It was thrilling going to another country, even briefly. The choir trip fulfilled several romantic desires, including the opportunity to wear a long formal, which we did for our performances. Music and religion fed some of my romantic and ecstatic inclinations. Clearly, the cello and organ accompaniment to Haydn's *Creation* stirred my soul, and although I didn't know it, I was indebted to our choir director. This powerful, classical music made me associate church with a happy, thrilling place. It already was a safe place because my alcoholic father never came there. So school and church became two havens for me.

My next experience with death came when I was sixteen in 1955. That summer, two young high school athletes drowned in Pine Lake in my hometown. One was a star of our basketball team named Richard Hult and one was a young woman who also excelled at sports but whose name I've forgotten. Her body was caught in weeds at the lake and not found for several days. In retrospect, I think their not finding her body disturbed me as much as her death. Neither of them were personal friends from school or church, yet everyone in town was deeply touched by their deaths. The death of two strong young athletes was not in the natural order of things. While the newspaper posted stories about them for several days, I don't remember my family discussing this much. This may have been because of the "don't talk, don't feel" messages common in alcoholic families or because my parents were busy working. I do remember it being a general topic of conversation and consternation in the newspaper over the girl's body not being found right away. Hence the social comment. I don't remember viewing their bodies at the funeral homes or going to their funerals. I was saddened by their deaths but more mystified than deeply bereaved, since their deaths were not in the natural order of things.

Therefore, I was quite surprised a few years ago when the topic of the young man's death came up with an old La Porte elementary and high school friend named Pete Cumerford. He told me he had been confounded by Richard Hult's death. He had attended the same church as Richard, and he sought consolation from several ministers trying to understand it. None were able to satisfactorily answer his questions. Since he had a deep personal relationship with Richard, his death had a very profound effect on Peter. As a result, he suffered a crisis of faith when no minister assured him that Richard was in heaven. I didn't feel so overwhelmed, and when I was reading a scripture from Isaiah the other day, I realized why I wasn't so shaken. The passage from Isaiah 55:9 reads, "As the heavens are higher than the earth, so are my ways higher than your ways and my thoughts than your thoughts." I think in retrospect I must have thought something like this. I remember feeling saddened by their deaths but did not experience a crisis of faith. Today, I still believe some things are mysteries that I don't understand. Since I hadn't seen this La Porte friend for more than fifty years, I hadn't been aware of the impact Richard's death had had on him.

Now, I can see that his death for his family and friends was devastating. Since La Porte was a small town of twenty-five thousand, most people were supportive of both of these families. Everyone was concerned for them and did what they could to help. Still, in 1955, I didn't hear death's bell tolling for me in that experience because I didn't have a deep personal relationship to him.

During the next decade, I lived away from La Porte and was occupied with college, graduate school, marriage, and motherhood. I was cut off from information about the deaths of high school friends and relatives. I remember my mother telling me of my Grandma Johnson's death months after it happened. She knew I couldn't afford to return to La Porte for her funeral when I was in college, so she just didn't tell me about it till later. Also, my grandmother's death was in the natural order of things. She was in her seventies, so it wasn't a disaster. She had always appeared old and stern to me, so I didn't have a deep emotional attachment to her. It seemed normal that an old person like her would die. Today, I wouldn't consider someone in their seventies old, but that's the difference between youth and old age. During my twenties and even forties, seventy seemed old.

Decades later, a conversation with one cousin showed me that some of my cousins had deep and positive emotional attachments to our grandmother, and they had grieved for her. They were younger, still living in La Porte, had closer ties to her as children, and would have gone to her funeral. So their situation was different. My mother did not mention her mother's death again to me, so I never knew to what extent she grieved her mother's death. I sensed from visits to my Great-grandmother Iselman in the hospital in the mid 1950s that my mother was more emotionally attached to her grandmother than to her mother. But I may be wrong. I do remember my mother asking me to go to the hospital with her to visit her grandmother. As a teenager, I wasn't keen on visiting a dying person in the hospital, but since my mother asked me to go, I went. I didn't have much understanding of sickness and death nor of being supportive, but somehow I sensed my mom needed me with her.

The death of my father in January 1967 had more impact on me. I never thought of my dad as old. So, his death didn't strike me as in the "natural order of things." Indeed, I felt sad at his death, especially for my mother who had been married to him for more than thirty years. She felt tremendous loss. Yet I didn't feel devastated because his alcoholism had made him a hard man to be around. Instead, I felt relief that I'd never feel threatened or shamed by him again. Reading a book called *The Invisible Thread* by Laura Schroff recently, I noticed her description of relief when her abusive, alcoholic father died. I could relate to that. The fear underpinning alcoholic families is a terrible burden. The threat of violence is traumatic, so the death of the alcoholic can be welcome.

In the 1960s, Americans were horrified at the assassinations of John F. Kennedy; his brother, Robert F. Kennedy; Martin Luther King, Jr.; and later Malcolm X. Few knew these men personally, yet we admired them and felt tremendous loss at their murders. Their widows and children were constant reminders of their deaths. On a deeper level, these events signaled a loss of innocence in American culture.

Musings on Death

Decades later, we witnessed the killing of little children at Sandy Hook Elementary School in Newtown, Connecticut, in December 2012 by a mass shooter. Unfortunately, this was only the first of many such events. It has been followed by too many others, including those at Uvalde, Texas, and Nashville, Tennessee. A memorial at Sandy Hook was erected ten years later, and the words of President Barack Obama echo as powerfully now as they did then:

> Here in Newtown, I come to offer the love and prayers of a nation. I am very mindful that mere words cannot match the depths of your sorrow, nor can they heal your wounded hearts. I can only hope it helps for you to know that you're not alone in your grief; that our world too has been torn apart … (as quoted in the *Lincoln Journal Star*, Dave Collins, "Sandy Hook school memorial opens," Monday, November 14, 2022, p. A7).

Sad to say, these people were not left to be comforted in their grief because conspiracy tormenters began disparaging the event. One of these detractors has been taken to court and sentenced to pay the survivors. As though money could make up for the pain he has inflicted on the poor parents! These conspiracy theorists threaten our country with their fake news. Moreover, gun makers and the National Rifle Association (NRA) work to prevent effective gun restrictions, and we are all threatened by the availability of AR-15s and other automatic weapons, even more so by concealed-carry laws in many states, including Nebraska.

The murder of George Floyd by four policemen in Minneapolis, Minnesota, on May 25, 2020, has also darkened our hearts. This slow murder of a man pinned on the ground and unable to breathe was filmed by a bystander and broadcast on TV in the USA and all around the world. However, this murder led to the movement Black Lives Matter and to the awareness of racism among many white Americans, including myself. Our complicity in destructive, systemic racism has shown its ugliness. All too often we hear of a young black man stopped at a stop sign and subsequently killed by the police. We hear of the overcrowding of our prisons, especially with people of color, who are vastly overrepresented in the prison population. Our hearts grieve, and we wonder what we can do to redeem our country from the scourge of racism. All of a sudden it has become obvious what our sins of commission and omission have been, lo these many decades.

Divorce and the Death of a Marriage

The most devastating loss for me was the death of my marriage by divorce in 1979 when I was thirty-nine years old. I heard a psychologist say that getting divorced is more painful than having a spouse die. That impressed me, since I was having a hard time adjusting to being divorced. He explained that a widow could continue thinking of her husband as a loving person, but when one divorced, one had to reevaluate one's former spouse and recognize that the dream person one thought one had married was seriously flawed. It was a time of disillusionment.

Indeed, this was the first crisis in my life. My father's death had been sad but not catastrophic. Likewise, no one in my immediate family had suffered serious, lingering illness. We had all been remarkably healthy and remained that way for decades. Before getting divorced, I had tried talking to my husband about marriage counseling, but he refused. I wanted him to be more loving and attentive to me, but he didn't want to renegotiate our marriage. I was dumbfounded when he preferred divorce to change, but he did. Moreover, I had grown increasingly jealous of attention he paid to one of his students, and I didn't like being that way. I was tired of being angry and frustrated with not getting my needs met. He got a lawyer, so I didn't think I needed one. We didn't have any money, and we had no property to divide since we had always lived a frugal, minimalist life. At the time of our divorce, I was also feeling apprehensive about writing my dissertation. No one in my family had ever done that. I felt adrift and alone. The one place I thought of fleeing was Iowa City, where I still had friends. I knew I couldn't stand being in Kansas City, seeing John with his student lover. That would have driven me mad. I didn't think of returning to my hometown to live with my mother. What sort of job would I get with an M.A. in Russian history in La Porte, Indiana? Nothing I could think of.

So, I fled to the University of Iowa, where I could support myself as a teaching assistant. Initially, I had had a fellowship at the university, so I had never taught and thought I should try it, since I now had to support myself. It was disappointing but understandable that my son wanted to stay in Kansas City with his father. He was going into his junior year in high school, and he didn't want to leave his friends and the neighborhood which he had become accustomed to. Still, that was another blow, and I felt guilty and ashamed. What kind of a mother was I to leave her son? I was a woman trying to survive, escaping a marriage in which I felt I couldn't breathe.

So under the pretext of wanting to finish my dissertation, I returned to Iowa City. As a teaching assistant, I could support myself. It turned out I liked teaching and was good at it. Not so good at dealing with my broken heart or finishing my dissertation in a timely manner. It took several years to mend my broken heart and complete my PhD.

Fortunately for me, God provided a kind but tough-minded priest, Anne Baker at Trinity Episcopal Church, to help me. I sought her out because I knew she would challenge me more than our male priest, who was a glad-hander. I suspected that if I'd gone to see him he would have patted me on the head and said "There, there, you'll be OK." In contrast, Anne gave me provocative books to read. I remember one called *Diving Deep and Surfacing*. I didn't understand all of it. However, the title suggested my plight. I too was diving deep into a new life without my beloved. I felt naked and vulnerable. But as the title suggests, I was surviving, eventually even flourishing. I consulted other therapists, but none helped. I wasn't very open about my pain. The habit of living in denial that I had learned in my childhood was hard to break. But Anne was patient and kind. I remember her saying, "I didn't think you would ever get divorced from that man." Slowly, I gave up some of my self-loathing and began to experience new self-esteem as I learned to appreciate my skills as a teacher and made new friends.

In some ways, this experience of losing my old self and creating a new one presaged my fears about death when I had my operation several years ago. The fear of losing myself is incredibly strong. Understanding the transformation that death provides is astounding and unsettling. It takes a while to process. We have to give ourselves time, space, and support to process this.

The Invisible Thread

By invisible thread, I mean God's design or providence linking us to other people, books (including the Scriptures), and events in our lives. One example in my life in the 1980s was meeting Betty Wetlaufer at Trinity Church in Iowa City. Betty was an older woman, a widow with grown children and grandchildren in Iowa City. She was deeply religious and a seeker. She came to Wednesday night communion service at Trinity Church, where we met. Eventually, we ended up having supper together after church and becoming friends. Betty was taking a course in the Religion Department about women in the Old Testament. She was involved in it and became friends with one of the young students in the course. This student invited her home to dinner at Christus House where she lived. This was a group of young Christians, both men and women, who lived communally while attending the university. Betty was impressed by them and thought I might like living there. So, I too went to dinner and was duly impressed with the community. The group gathered every evening after supper and participated in Christian sharing. Students took turns cooking for each other and leading evening programs.

After visiting with them, I felt drawn to joining the group. The two houses provided bedrooms for members at a very reasonable price. People took responsibility for grocery shopping and cooking two nights per month. I liked this aspect of communal living since I had enjoyed cooking for fifteen years while a housewife. I had experience making granola and made huge batches of it for the community. I liked the idea of using one stove to cook for seventeen people. Even before climate change, conserving resources made sense to me. As an armchair socialist, I appreciated living in community and saving resources. It represented a dream come true. I liked the idea of sharing and cooperating. At Christus House, we also participated in cleaning the common areas of the two buildings plus the laundry room in the basement. No one entered into the cleaning activity with much gusto until an Italian student came to live there one summer. He actually cleaned the basement with great gusto and put the rest of us to shame. It was an interesting summer. I had won a fifteen-speed bike in a political raffle, and I didn't really know how to ride it. I offered to let the Italian student use it, and he was very pleased to zoom around on it. Unlike him, I preferred walking to the library to do my research and writing. As a PhD student, I had a lovely office of my own on the third floor to work on my dissertation. There too God provided an invisible thread to two other new people in my life—one young fellow studying for a PhD in religion and a French-speaking Belgian woman studying in the Business Department. Both of them became friends for several years as we finished our studies.

At Christus House, I found my anger at my divorce dissipating. Interacting with new friends, I found myself healing. Being around loving, prayerful young people provided a form of "new and unending life" that the Episcopal prayer book suggests for us during communion. Instead of ranting and raving about my former husband in my mind as I jogged in the mornings, I found myself enjoying my time running along the Iowa River. Nature also helped heal me. Christus House offered a new way of life. Living and praying with like-minded people changed me. I no longer felt so angry and cheated by my former husband. I was able to move from the past to the present. I'm sure this was the work of the Holy Spirit intervening in my life and showing me a new way to live—communally and lovingly. This doesn't mean there were never disagreements at the house. Seventeen people with different intellectual interests, religious backgrounds, and origins (including Thailand, Indonesia, Taiwan, Hong Kong, and Puerto Rico) were bound to have some misunderstandings. But the Holy Spirit and our thoughtful leader, Gretchen Bingea, helped us live in relative peace and harmony.

Still nursing my broken heart the first summer I lived at Christus House, I started reading John Donne's *Devotions upon Emergent Occasions*. At the time, I couldn't understand why I was attracted to these writings. Maybe it was because I was dealing with the death of my marriage, and these writings comforted me. In retrospect, it appears the invisible hand of God led me to Christus House and John Donne. Both experiences helped heal and renew me.

Glancing at a book a friend recently gave me called *Dreams and Spiritual Growth: A Christian Approach to Dreamwork* by Louis M. Savary, Patricia H. Berne, and Strephon Kaplan Williams, I noticed a helpful definition of spirituality. The authors defined it as "one's way of responding to God's call, a style of living that is open to the energies of God's spirit." This is certainly one of the things that happened to me while living at Christus House. I developed a better way of being open to the energies of God's spirit in the people living there and to God's revelations in Donne's meditations. I was ready for new life and it happened there. I had been marginally aware of Christus House when I first came to Iowa City in 1962, and if I had checked it out instead of being mildly dismissive of it, my life would have unfolded differently. But for the sake of falling in love with my former husband and the birth of our son, Martin, I'm glad that God blessed me in those ways instead of developing a life at Christus House the first time. It shows that God continues to work in our lives and in the choices we make. God doesn't desert us when we choose one path over another.

Rereading John Donne's *Devotions upon Emergent Occasions* recently, I found them very comforting. All together he wrote twenty-three devotions. His most famous phrases, "For Whom the Bell Tolls" and "No Man Is an Island," are from Devotion 17. There are a few other phrases of Donne's that I'd also like to share from Devotion 17. He writes:

> Perchance he for whom this bell tolls may be so ill, as that he Knows not it tolls for him; and perchance I may think myself so much better than I am ... and I know not that. (Donne, p. 107)

He adds:

> As therefore the bell that rings to a sermon calls not upon the preacher only, but upon the congregation to come, so this bell calls us all; but how much more me, who am brought so near the door by this sickness.... The bell doth toll for him that thinks it doth;

and though it intermit again, yet from that minute that that occasion wrought upon him, he is united to God.

Then his famous and comforting words:

No man is an island, entire of itself; every man is a piece of the continent, a part of the main. If a clod be washed away by the sea, Europe is the less, as well as if a promontory were ... any man's death diminishes me, because I am involved in mankind, and therefore never send to know for whom the bell tolls; it tolls for thee. (Donne, pp. 108–109)

In a prayer following this meditation, Donne thanks God for speaking to him in nature, in his heart, Scriptures, animals, even in the sound of a sad funeral bell. He realizes that death is the wages of sin, so it is due to him, as death is the end of sickness it belongs to him. He also concludes that he need not doubt God's forgiveness, nor his infinite mercy. He is aware of his own demerits but prefers to wrap himself up in the merits of Jesus who breathes inward comfort into his heart. Donne asks God to receive his soul into God's kingdom and unite him in the communion of saints if this be his time to die (see Donne, pp. 112–113). In Meditation XVIII, Donne dwells upon the benefit of hearing the bell toll for someone because he benefited from that man's death to the extent that the bell reminded him to pray for his own soul as well as that of the deceased (Donne, 114–116). So, we too hear an echo in others' deaths and their funerals, which calls us to pray not only for the soul of the deceased but for ourselves as well.

One final quotation from Donne is from a statement he made when he thought he was dying. It reminded me of some of our thoughts during COVID. In Meditation V, he wrote that the solitude imposed on one during an infectious disease is not normal. We were not made to be alone. He prayed, "Thy kingdom come, thy will be done. Prosper me and relieve me, in thy way, in thy time, and in thy manner" (Donne, Meditation V, pp. 30–31, 34–35). During COVID, these words also rang true. In old age, I often realize we are not meant to be alone, and sometimes we feel more willing to serve in God's way, time, and manner. In Meditation VI, he writes that fearing God, we don't have to fear others, or even death.

Lately, I've begun to see some similarities between youth and old age. During both seasons of our lives, we may feel uncertainty and dread. For youth it may be uncertainty or even dread about the future; for old people these feelings may center on death. When discussing this observation with my friend Michael Johnson, he mentioned a popular song he heard in Quebec in 1990. It was titled "Le Trac de Lendemain," or "The Dread of Tomorrow." This suggests that young people there too felt dread about the future. In her book *On My Own at 107*, Sadie Delany mentions that her sister Bessie thought she could choreograph her death, that is, eliminate the uncertainty of when or how it would occur. Sadie thought we can't do this. (See Sarah L. Delany with Amy Hill Heath, *On My Own at 107: Reflections on Life without Bessie*, Harper San Francisco, 1997, p. 41.) Musing on death, Sadie hoped to die in her sleep and be brave. But she suspected she'd be just as scared as the next person (Delany, p. 69). I suspect I'll be like this too. I imagine the only way we can control our death is if we commit suicide.

Musings on Death

In her book *Winter Grace*, Fischer draws some parallels between old age and adolescence. She writes that old people and teens may be similarly afflicted with questions of self-worth, self-esteem, loneliness, isolation, boredom, and lack of status and jobs. All ages experience grief, loss, failure, limitations, and reflections on death. For some youth, it ends in suicide. For some elders, it also ends in suicide. But she notes that in old age, we are generally better equipped to deal with boredom, loneliness, and isolation. In old age our experience of loss is more common and perhaps less overwhelming. She sees loneliness as rooted in our longing for God. In solitude we hear the voice of God in the stillness, in which we can contemplate God's presence (Fischer, pp. 19, 31–32). Until reading her book, I hadn't realized the similarities between these two ages.

Death and Curiosity

Over the years, I've noticed that death and funerals have had an uneven impact on me. My mother died in October 1997 at age eighty-five. While this was sad, it wasn't overwhelming. Her health had declined, and her death seemed in the natural order, as did that of an elderly aunt and uncle the same year. When my mother was in a nursing home in El Paso, Texas, where I was teaching at the time, I used to wonder about her. She was so emaciated and couldn't eat, but doctors had put a feeding tube in her stomach, which kept her marginally alive. Her quality of life was very low. She had regressed in her dementia, thinking I was her sister. She didn't seem to be in pain, but she wasn't very alive. I thought to myself as I prayed in the elevator going to see her each day: "I wonder why God is keeping her alive." I just didn't understand. Eventually, I decided that life and death are mysteries that we can't always fathom. Then, I just accepted her situation, since she did. A few months later mother died peacefully, which was a blessing.

More haunting was the death of my former husband earlier that same year. At fifty-seven, his death was not in the natural order. Nor was Princess Diana's the same summer. When I found myself crying uncontrollably at Diana's televised funeral, I wondered what that was about. Then I realized that my tears may also have been for my former husband, my gardener, a neighbor, and my Aunt Gladys, who had all died earlier that year, as well as for those slowly dwindling away like my colleague Ellery Schalk and my mother.

As I've recently been thinking about illness, aging, and death, especially my own death, I've noticed some changes in my attitude. Whereas when I was in my seventies, I found death uninteresting, frightening, or upsetting, and tried not thinking about it much, in my eighties, my attitude has changed, and I feel more able to look at darkness, within and without. Maybe COVID has forced us all to do this.

But I know today I'm more curious about death, more open to thinking about it and speculating on it. Indeed, when I went to visit my old friend Miriam Gelfand in Iowa City before COVID, we sometimes talked about death. Our conversations were not morbid. Her husband had died several years earlier, and she was in her nineties, so death was not so far away. Death seemed interesting to her and to me, especially after we saw a film about Shakespeare and the death of one of his children. This may have sparked one of our discussions; I'm not sure.

Musings on Death

Recently, I had a vision about death. In the vision, I saw a really tired figure. She was so tired, she sat down and expired. Then, I realized that is what death can be like. Feeling really tired and then just letting go. It didn't hurt.

In the vision, I called my good friend at Pioneer House, Corlee, to come help me. I knew I wasn't well. I just hadn't known I was going to die. It was all very peaceful. No struggle to stay alive. Just letting go. Interesting when we are ready to let go. In retrospect, letting go may have been about my move to Eastmont and the letting go of my life at Pioneer House, not necessarily my physical death.

I don't feel like I'm ready to die yet. But much of the time I feel that I will be OK with the process. I'm glad I've been able to write this book on aging and spirituality. It's helped me. When I feel overwhelmed by the death and illness of friends, I find I am more able to take them to the Lord in prayer. Then, I don't feel so overwhelmed.

Chapter IV

Comfort in Death: Funerals

Part of aging involves attending more funerals of friends, family members, and acquaintances. Going to funerals can be comforting and deepen our spirituality. One for a fellow parishioner in the spring of 2022 combined gravitas and comfort. The scriptures included the one I began this book with from 2 Corinthians 4:16–18 but was a fuller quotation:

> So we do not lose heart. Even though our outer nature is wasting away, our inner nature is being renewed day by day. For this slight momentary affliction is preparing us for an eternal weight of glory beyond all measure because we look not at what can be seen but at what cannot be seen, for what can be seen is temporary but what cannot be seen is eternal.

The music at the funeral was also touching, especially Bach's "Jesu, Joy of Man's Desiring" and the hymns "Just a Closer Walk with Thee" and "I Sing a Song of the Saints of God." Sitting there, I thought "the familiar can be comforting and sad at the same time." Some of the words were also hopeful. As the priest movingly sang the lyrics of the first hymn, the congregation joined in the chorus:

> Just a closer walk with Thee,
> Grant it, Jesus, is my plea,
> Daily walking close to Thee,
> Let it be, dear Lord, let it be.

This music warmed my soul. Indeed, tears which had been under control earlier, rolled down my cheeks. Crying can be such a release. It was a moment of grace, drawing the entire congregation together. By the time of the last hymn, about being the saints of God, I felt like I really wanted more than ever to be one too. I felt like rededicating my baptismal vows and felt part of the community of saints. I felt sad at the death of a friend but also lifted up for the life I have yet to live.

Comfort may also come from the remembrances of family and friends. This happened during this funeral when the son of the deceased spoke lovingly of his father. It made me wish every parent had a child like that to pay tribute to them in such a way.

The commendation from the Episcopal *Book of Common Prayer* was trenchant:

> Give rest, O Christ, to your servant with your saints, where sorrow and pain are no more, neither sighing, but life everlasting.
> You only are immortal, the creator and maker of mankind; and we are mortal formed of the earth and to earth shall we return. For so did you ordain when you created us, saying "You are dust and to dust you shall return." All of us go down to the dust, yet even at the grave we make our song: Alleluia, alleluia, alleluia.

Into your hands, O merciful Savior, we commend your servant ____. Acknowledge, we humbly beseech you, a sheep of your own fold, a lamb of your own flock, a sinner of your own redeeming. Receive him into the arms of your mercy, into the blessed rest of everlasting peace, and into the glorious company of the saints in light. Amen.

This prayer left me at peace, making me think that death can help us appreciate life. Just as Jesus triumphed over death by rising from the dead, we feel similarly lifted up by the ritual of a funeral. We vow to live our lives more intentionally and with greater awareness and compassion.

Musing upon this funeral a few days later, I thought of how I have changed my behavior after funerals. While I used to go to a funeral to pay my respects to the deceased, have a good cry, and to find comfort for myself, I find that I still do these but that I spend more time afterward praying for the bereaved left behind. This fall I added a section to my daily prayers that includes the names of those who have recently lost a parent, child, spouse, or loved one. This reminded me of the admonition in one of the communion prayers that we come to the communion table not for solace only but for strength and service too.

The funeral for another St. Mark's parishioner, Don Steinegger, a year later also comforted me. Both were Episcopal services, but the program and liturgy were slightly different. Don's wife, Susan, told me he had crafted his service before his dementia became acute, and it was a very touching service. His featured the prayer of St. Francis of Assisi, which reminded me of my mother, who also loved that prayer. I include it here:

Lord, make me an instrument of your peace.
Where there is hatred, let me sow love;
Where there is injury, pardon;
Where there is doubt, faith;
Where there is despair, hope;
Where there is darkness, light;
And where there is sadness, joy.

O Divine Master, grant that I may not so much seek
To be consoled as to console;
To be understood as to understand
To be loved as to love.
For it is in giving that we receive;
It is in pardoning that we are pardoned;
And it is in dying that we are born to eternal life.
       Amen

There were many such touching parts. One that stood out was the beginning, which read: "For if we have life, we are alive in the Lord, and if we die, we die in the Lord. So, then, whether we live or die we are the Lord's." What could be more reassuring than these words?

A reading from Psalm 90:12 encouraged us "to count our days that we may gain a wise heart."

We all seem to need this reminder from time to time. The Prayers of the People also contained comforting passages:

> "For our brother Don, let us pray to our Lord Jesus Christ who said, "I am Resurrection, and I am Life."
> Lord, you consoled Martha and Mary in their

distress; draw near to us who mourn for Don, and dry the tears of those who weep.

You wept at the grave of Lazarus, your friend; comfort us in our sorrow.

You raised the dead to life: give to our brother eternal life.

You promised paradise to the thief who repented; bring our brother to the joys of heaven.

Our brother was washed in Baptism and anointed with the Spirit; give him fellowship with all your saints.

He was nourished with your Body and Blood; grant him a place at the table in your heavenly kingdom.

Comfort us in our sorrows at the death of our brother, let our faith be our consolation, and eternal life our hope.

Father of all, we pray to you for Don, and for all those whom we love but see no longer. Grant to them eternal rest. Let light perpetual shine upon them. May his soul and the souls of all the departed, through the mercy of God, rest in peace.

                                             Amen

This wasn't the end of the service but the end of many special prayers, since communion followed.

Another funeral occurred at our church in April, that of a beloved friend, Roger Wait. It too aroused a lot of emotion. I had known Roger as a friend and a pew mate for eight years. He had introduced me to the Healing Order of St. Luke in Lincoln, and I was so grateful to him for that monthly meeting and healing service. So his funeral, while not unexpected at eighty-eight, was still daunting. I didn't really feel comforted until late in the service when we were taking communion, and words of the prayer revived me:

> ... For to your faithful people, O Lord, life is changed, not ended, and when our mortal body lies in death, there is prepared for us a dwelling place eternal in the heavens.

Likewise the prayer of commendation was consoling:

> "Give rest, O Christ, to your servant with your saints, where sorrow and pain are no more, neither sighing, but life everlasting.
>
> ... For so did you ordain when you created me saying, "You are dust, and to dust you shall return." All of us go down to the dust; yet even at the grave we make our song: Alleluia, alleluia, alleluia.

It was a solace to hear that while the mortal body dies, there is a place eternal in the heavens prepared for our soul, and our song remains "Alleluia." Equally comforting were the words of my Pioneer House friend Michael Johnson, who said he thought heaven was like a foreign country we had never yet visited. That was very consoling. We had been talking of Roger's death and funeral while waiting for a ride to church, when Michael uttered those thoughtful words. I find my friend Michael often has helpful words. He was the one who reminded me years earlier of the dictum "the natural order of things." At eighty-eight, Roger's death was in the natural order of things and as such not tragic. So while I regretted his death, I didn't mourn too long.

Musing about these funerals reminded me that death brings us together—not only our church family at St. Mark's Episcopal Church but other groups as well. Three events were a remembrance service for former members of Pioneer House on September 9, 2022; my brother's ceremony at St. Mark's; and of course the much bigger event of Queen Elizabeth II's death and funeral a week later.

Remembrance Service at Pioneer House

A few weeks before Queen Elizabeth II died, some friends and I at Pioneer House had been talking about having a remembrance service for some members who had died during COVID but for whom no funerals or services had been held during the two-year restrictions. Corlee Pralle, Michael Johnson, and I had discussed this subject off and on for some time but had never decided on a date until early September. Finally we decided to have a remembrance service to pay our last respects to several former members of Pioneer House on September 9, 2022. Corlee offered her apartment as the venue, and she played some hymns on her organ. She also made homemade ice cream to serve to everyone after the service. We agreed that Corlee would open the service with a hymn, followed by Michael reading some prayers from the Episcopal *Book of Common Prayer* burial service, and I would read appropriate scriptures from the Old and New Testaments. Michael xeroxed ten copies of the prayers, so we could follow along in our short service. I read the scriptures, and after the last prayer, we spoke about some of the people we had remembered. Then we began to add other names to the list. It was surprising that so many had moved away or died during the last few years and those we had overlooked and forgotten.

It turned out to be a memorable and pleasant evening. Although it lacked the pomp and circumstance of Queen Elizabeth's funeral held a week later, it was a moving occasion, proving once again that death can bring people together. One of the prayers I found particularly comforting contained the following words:

> O God of grace and glory, we remember before you this day our brothers and sisters [whose names were read]. We thank you for giving them to us, their family, and friends to know and to love as companions on our earthly pilgrimage. In your boundless compassion, console us who mourn. Give us faith to see in death the gate of eternal life, so that in quiet confidence we may continue our course on earth, until, by your call, we are reunited with those who have gone before; through Jesus Christ our Lord. Amen.

Now more than ever, it's good to hear words like "console us" and "quiet confidence." With political and climate turmoil, it's good to hear of quiet confidence.

The scripture from Isaiah comforted us. Verse 8 from chapter 25 read "The Lord All Powerful will destroy the power of death and wipe away all tears." Likewise, Revelation 17:7 also speaks of God wiping away all our tears. All together, the scriptures and prayers consoled us. Like the psalmists and prophets, we find that in the midst of sadness and affliction, God comforts us.

Death of Family during COVID

During COVID, it was unwise to hold funerals or memorial services for the dead, and few were held. This made grieving and saying goodbye to our loved ones more difficult. Indeed, of the many friends at Pioneer House who died during COVID, only two had services. So it was hard to process the loss of loved ones for two years. I also experienced the loss of two cousins, Jane and Sandy, as well as my brother, Walter. My brother died the end of July 2020 but of natural causes, not COVID. Since COVID was flaring all over the country, we couldn't have a service for him in Tucson then. We thought we'd be able to do it a year hence, but that didn't happen. I arranged a service of remembrance in Lincoln, but none of his friends from Arizona or Oregon could come because of COVID travel restrictions. One reason we could have the service was because we had it in our church courtyard. It was a great solace to me to have friends from Lincoln with me, but I was aware that his caregivers and friends in Tucson were still grieving and unable to attend to be comforted. I wrote a letter honoring my brother and sent it to them, but it wasn't the same as a live ceremony. So, COVID hit the aged especially hard. We experienced a great deal of loss in the death of friends and relations without the traditional rituals to mourn them.

Comfort in Death: Funerals

Funeral of Queen Elizabeth II

The death and funeral of Queen Elizabeth II certainly showed on a grand scale how death can bring people together. Heads of state, estranged members of the royal family, and millions of people in the United Kingdom and the entire world joined together to "pay their respects" to the late queen. Many Americans joined in for several days via television. I was amazed at the hundreds of thousands who queued in Scotland to pay their respects in churches there. More amazing were the long lines lasting ten or more hours of people in London queuing to honor the queen prior to her funeral. It was touching that some young people queued for their grandparents who couldn't. They also wanted to honor the queen who, among other things, had represented decency and public service for seventy years.

As the events of Elizabeth's funeral revealed, she had provided detailed instructions for her service, including the choice of hymns, venue, and service. As head of state and head of the Anglican Church, Elizabeth was aware of the hole she was leaving in the hearts of many of her subjects. She planned a meaningful and impressive ceremony at Westminster Abbey and a more sober and somber service at St. George's Chapel, Windsor Castle. The rites, rituals, and rich vestments of the officiating priests provided pageantry at Westminster. The stained glass of the abbey lifted the soul, and the organ, choir, brass, and drums deeply moved us, helping us process our feelings of grief. After the final trumpet fanfare, the piping by a Scottish bagpiper was haunting yet consoling. The queen's thoughtfulness in including ministers from the Church of Scotland and other English churches showed her understanding of diversity in the UK and her gracious concern for inclusion. The short homily by the archbishop touchingly compared the queen's life of service to that of Jesus. His invitation to all watching to renew their service to family, friends, and others was also a reminder to us to emulate Jesus' example of service.

One of the most moving parts of the committal service at St. George's Chapel was the removing of the gold orb, scepter, and crown from her casket and placing them on the altar. This symbolized the end of Elizabeth's rule. The end of her power. The end of her earthly life. These rites and rituals reminded me of the scripture that "naked we come into the world, and naked leave it." The golden orb, scepter, and crown would be used later for the coronation of her son, Charles III.

Hymns and Death

A great source of comfort about death can be found in hymns. Two of the hymns at Elizabeth's service, "All My Hope in God Is Founded" and "Christ Is Made the Sure Foundation," stirred me with their lilting melodies and words. Some of the verses of two other hymns have resonated with me about death. One is "If You But Trust in God to Guide You," and the second is 'Lord, Dismiss Us with Your Blessing." I'm sure there are many more. These are just two that "spoke to me." The fourth verse of "Lord, Dismiss Us" reads as follows:

> Savior when your love shall call us
> From our struggling pilgrim way,
> Let no fear of death appall us

Comfort in Death: Funerals

Glad your summons to obey.
May we ever, may we ever
Reign with you in endless day.

I especially like the words "Let no fear of death appall us." I think the more I read and reflect about death and dying, it appalls me less. When we're younger, it's easy for death to frighten and appall us.

Words in the hymn "If You But Trust in God to Guide You" touched me, especially the first and last verses:

If you but trust in God to guide you
And place your confidence in him,
You'll find him always there beside you,
To give you hope and strength within.
For those who trust God's changeless love
Build on the rock that will not move.

Sing, pray, and keep his ways unswerving.
Offer your service faithfully,
And trust his word, though undeserving,
You'll find his promise true to be.
God never will forsake in need
The soul that trusts in him indeed.

The words that strike me as moving in this hymn are those about trusting God, finding God beside us, and God giving us hope and strength; likewise, the final words, that God doesn't forsake the souls that trust in him in need. These words and the tune are consoling.

Prayers for the Dead in Other Christian Traditions

A minister at the Christian Church named Dennis Swensen kindly sent me some prayers of comfort that he had offered at funerals for members of his church. His prayers were extemporaneous and not based on a liturgy as those in the Episcopal, Lutheran, Roman Catholic, and Orthodox traditions are. For one member of his congregation, he prayed:

> Heavenly Father, at a time of deeply felt loss, we turn to you for comfort. We glorify you for creating each one of us in your image. We acknowledge your sovereign wisdom in setting limits to our life on earth. And yet the departure of someone we love reminds us of the shortness of our own time on earth. Remind us again this morning of your love and grace demonstrated through the life of your son Jesus. Amen.

Later he prayed:

> Heavenly Father, we remember how your son Jesus reached out to touch those who were grieving, and we remember that His touch was healing. Come now and touch this family and those friends so that grief may be cleansing and healing may begin. You know our loneliness. Send us the warmth of your friendship. You know our regrets. Send us the balm of forgiveness and renewal. You know the emptiness of our hearts. Give us a new song to sing, a new day to live, and a new joy to behold. We thank you now for the gifts you

shared through D's life. We cherish those gifts and ask that you remind us of the goodness of her life, so that our own lives might be enriched. Now may the grace of the Lord Jesus Christ, the love of God the Father, and the communion of the Holy Spirit be with you all. Amen.

Another prayer Dennis enclosed offered these consoling words:

Gracious Father, in this hour of need, keep us close to you and to one another. We thank you for G and his life. It is not easy for us to say our goodbyes, and the days can sometimes be hard for us. We have shared some of our memories of G this afternoon. So, we ask you to bless and comfort the hurt in our hearts. Give us the energy we need to live the rest of our lives well. Help us not to move into bitterness and alienation with you or with one another. We can get through this difficult time in our lives as you give us your strength to sustain us. Grant us peace. Amen.

Celebration of Life Services

Celebration of life services differ from traditional funerals in some ways. One of the differences is in the choice of music. Whereas traditional funerals usually feature hymns and classical music, celebration of life services seem to focus on modern music. I've been to two services lately which featured the song "Precious Lord, Take my Hand." One of them used a recording by Elvis Presley. Apparently the deceased was a fan of Elvis. I hadn't realized this. So we learn about our friends even after they have died. Another song was "How Great Thou Art." Both are uplifting. Sermons or talks at these services are usually upbeat too: less about the resurrection, more about God's grace. Often there are tributes to the dead by their relatives. One of the most moving was the letters of two sisters about their dead sister. A friend and I agreed that it was one of the most touching services we had ever experienced. It told us about all three sisters.

The most unusual funeral I attended lately was one in the Greek Orthodox Church in Lincoln. In this tradition, resurrection is celebrated, and the open casket with the deceased is given an honorable place in the front of the church all during the service. At the end of the service, members of the congregation were invited to process around the church to bid farewell to the deceased. Some kissed the body, others crossed themselves and the body, others showed other forms of reverence. It was a very restorative and unusual service for me. Some Southern Baptist churches also conduct funeral services with an open casket.

Prayers for the Dead in Other Religious Traditions

As I thought of asking a Jewish friend to read my writing on aging and spirituality, I suddenly realized that I had included only Christian prayers for the dead. I knew that Jews also said a prayer for the dead called Kaddish, a thirteenth-century prayer whose name means "holy." So, I asked Steve Blum, and he translated these prayers for me. According to Steve, who was raised in the Jewish tradition, Jews do not mention the dead person's name but proclaim the greatness of God. By saying it, mourners show that even in their loss, God is great. Also, they need a quorum of ten to be with the grieving person to say the prayer in a community. Usually, Kaddish is said for eleven months following a death. The rhythmic cadences of Kaddish are soothing to mourners, and over the years they say it at Yahrzeit and at Yizkor to remember loved ones. They say the prayer as a community so that no one is alone in their mourning.

The translation of Kaddish:

> Magnified and sanctified is the great name of God throughout the world, which was created according to Divine will. May the rule of peace be established speedily in our time, unto us and unto the entire household of Israel. And let us say: Amen.
>
> May God's great name be praised throughout all eternity. Glorified and celebrated, lauded and praised, acclaimed and honored, extolled and exalted ever be the name of the Holy One, far beyond all song and psalm, beyond all hymns of glory which mortals can offer. And let us say: Amen.
>
> May there be abundant peace from heaven, with life's goodness for us and for all thy people Israel. And let us say: Amen.
>
> May the One who brings peace to the universe bring peace to us and to all the people Israel. And let us say: Amen.

An Indian friend, whom I met in Lincoln while she was completing her MA in English, told me via email about Indian burial customs. She said that in India Muslims bury their dead, but other religious groups, including Hindus, Jains, Sikhs, and others, cremate theirs. A Hindu, she told me the following about their funeral customs. Apparently it is sons who cremate the dead family members. Chants are said, including the following: "Ram Naam Satya Hai" (May the name of Ram live/be true forever). The day after cremation, the family gathers the ashes and goes to a holy river, often the Ganges, where the ashes are poured into the river. Some worshipping occurs there before and after the ritual. On the third day, a "wake" is held, where friends gather and some speak about the late person. Sometimes this is accompanied by a priest reciting couplets from the "Gita" because that is where Lord Krishna speaks about the ephemeral nature of life. There is a fascinating perspective on life and death in the Gita. On the twelfth day after a death, the mourning period ends, marked by a feast. This feast is now discouraged, as it means a huge unnecessary expenditure and was probably started by Brahmins (the priestly caste). Although not strictly observed, the bereaved family does not celebrate festivals for a year. (Source: Madhamunti Gupta, near Delhi, India.) An Anglo/Indian Christian told me that they bury or cremate their dead in India. Their prayers and services are often traditional or old-fashioned compared to contemporary America. Some refrain from celebrations for a year after the death of a beloved. (Conversation with Harold Mondol, summer 2023.)

I don't have any personal friends who are Muslim, but when I looked up their burial customs and prayers on Google, here's what I found. First the dead body is washed by members of the

Comfort in Death: Funerals

same gender in one's family. The body is wrapped in a simple, modest, white cloth. Then prayers are said outside the mosque, usually by men. Burial of the body is with the head toward Mecca. Mourning varies: often a four-day mourning period is observed, except for widows who mourn for four months and ten days. Some customs vary according to region.

Prayers:

> O God, forgive our living and our dead, those who are present among us and those who are absent, our young and our old, our males and our females. O God, whoever You keep alive, keep him alive in Islam, and whoever You cause to die, cause him to die with faith. O God, do not deprive us of the reward and do not cause us to go astray after this. O God, forgive him and have mercy on him, keep him safe and sound and forgive him, honor his rest and ease his entrance; wash him with water and snow and hail, and cleanse him of sin as a white garment is cleansed of dirt. O God, give him a home better than his home and a family better than his family. O God, admit him to Paradise and protect him from the torment of the grave and the torment of Hellfire; make his grave spacious and fill it with light.

Chapter V

Significant Others during Aging and COVID

In his book *The Ninth Decade: An Octogenarian's Chronicle*, author Carl Klaus reminds us how important significant others are when we age. He discusses illness and ailments in great detail and credits nurses and doctors in Iowa City, Iowa, for helping him survive into his ninth decade. As a professor and founder of the nonfiction writing program at the University of Iowa, Klaus writes masterfully. It's a joy reading his work. Unlike Mary Pipher's *Women Rowing North*, in which she encourages us all to make more effort to live life meaningfully, Klaus's book reminds me more of Willa Cather's *Death Comes to the Archbishop*. In these books, decline and death are treated as natural phenomena we needn't fight or resist.

What I want to emphasize in this writing is not decline and death or using great effort to survive but rather the power of the Spirit to enrich our lives and make life worth living until the end. So my emphasis is less on discussing my medically significant others in Lincoln and more on showing how chronic illness made me aware of aging and the resulting groups that helped me deal with it.

As previously noted, my first diagnosis of bronchiectasis by my pulmonologist Dr. Fiedler led me to the Healing Ministry of

St. Luke's and Camp Farthest Out. My surgery for a prolapsed uterus and bladder led me to deal with my fear of death and dying and to an investigation of aging and spirituality with the help of my Jungian therapist Christine Grosh. Significant others I met at the women's clinic included Tammy Clark, nurse practitioner, and my surgeon, Dr. Tomjack. During COVID, an appreciation of my pharmacists at Walgreens increased.

Of course, my most significant others include my son, Martin Stack, and my daughter-in-law, Donna Schwisher. They are loving, kind, and helpful. Indeed, they also support my traveling and having a good time. When I went to Mexico a few years ago, they helped me book an Airbnb, which smoothed my way. Martin tried for years to get me to buy a smartphone. After I finally capitulated, he went with me to T-Mobile and bought the phone for me and even pays for it. He's a very generous son. When they come to visit me in Lincoln, they know I don't have a car, so they take me to the grocery store, hardware store, or wherever I need to go. They also treat me to the finest restaurants in Lincoln. Most of all, Martin calls me weekly to share what's happening in his life and to see how I am. I deeply appreciate his keeping in touch with me regularly.

I am also blessed with friends in Lincoln, Iowa City, Lithuania, and elsewhere who enrich my life. At Pioneer House, the cooperative where I used to live, there were a host of significant, supportive friends. Chief among them is my intellectual confidant and church friend Michael Johnson. Michael was a Spanish language professor at nearby Hastings College before he retired, so we share many common experiences of academe. Like me, he enjoys keeping up with the news and discussing political events. He also attends St. Mark's Episcopal

Church, so we also share a common religious heritage. He has offered me rides to church for a decade and to Whole Foods, where we often enjoyed lunch or dinner together and bought the groceries we needed. Michael is a great listener, and I have shared my sadness and conflicts as well as my happiness with him. We have had many authentic conversations about death and dying. I used to share my religious life with Beth Hemmer of Pioneer House until she died in January 2022. Her death is still a loss.

Other friends at Pioneer House offer community, friendship, prayers, and even rides when needed. There are so many, I can only name them in alphabetical order: Rafaella and Richard Bartels, Richard Burton, Bonnie and Rick Danke, Theresa Forsman, Kindra Foster, Kathy Linsenmyer, Bill O'Malley, Corlee Pralle, Joanne Santoro, Rayma Schrader, and Deb and John Swayze. When I decided to move to Eastmont, Corlee became a great helper and sustainer as I sorted my goods, and we packed them up together in boxes that resident Rita Stinner graciously lent me.

Another significant friend in Lincoln is Elaine Kruse, former French historian at Nebraska Wesleyan University. Elaine and I met in the 1980s at the University of Iowa, where we were both working on our dissertations. From time to time, I stayed with Elaine in Lincoln in the 1990s and 2000s. She is a gracious hostess and offers hospitality more effortlessly than most do. She belongs to First Lutheran Church and is someone with whom I share my faith as well my ideas about history and politics. She's also the friend who argues that we have had such rich and blessed lives that we don't have to be afraid to die. As academics, we have been able to travel a great deal, to teach meaningful courses in history, to read wonderful books, and to write meaningful articles and books. We are both "culture vultures," enjoying movies, concerts, and lectures together. She is generous with her time and has given me more rides to plays and concerts than I can remember. As a professor emeritus at NWU, she received free tickets to all the plays and musicals the university presents, and she freely shared these activities with me along with a needed ride. Over the years, she and Michael often provided me rides to my doctors' offices. So they are supportive of my health. Through Elaine I also became a member of the Lutheran women's book club, which is a delightful group that meets monthly to discuss books and celebrate members' birthdays at interesting Lincoln restaurants. Through Elaine, I can count these good women as friends too.

One of the amazing things about God's grace is the good people God sends to us in new places. Whereas I had become friends with our priest Roy Ball and his wife, Joke, in Lithuania, I found a new good friend and priest, Jerry Thompson, in Lincoln, Nebraska, when I moved here. Other church priests are Chuck Peek and Mary Hendricks (former priests) and Robert Magoola (current priest); deacons are Christine Grosh, Rich Kelly, and Roger Wait. St. Mark's church friends include Gwen Colgrove (former church secretary and helper), Mary Lutz, Mary Roseberry-Brown (prayer partner), Connie Backus Yoder (quilt maker and adult forum discussant), Bob Kuzelka, Susan and Mark Music, Loris Purtzer, Susan Robinson, Steve Blum, Steve Shively, Susan Steinegger, and Bob Stock (all adult forum discussants), Gwen Tilly (prayer partner), and Ross Mosier (office manager who has helped me run off copies of my writings and xeroxed items for me).

Recently, I had occasion to reflect on some significant others who enrich my life in downtown Lincoln. Although Lincoln is a city of three hundred thousand, it is a friendly place. Downtown merchants in particular often know your name and care about you as a customer. Three come to mind: Leslie Huerta, owner of Francie and Finch bookstore on 13th Street; Dean Settle of Metro Gallery, 13th and N Streets; and Scott Glenn, the owner of Executive Travel on O Street. I have frequented Leslie's bookshop for several years. She was really my neighborhood bookseller while I lived at Pioneer House. She's always friendly and helpful, offering customers hot cider and ginger cookies in the winter and a cool beverage in the summer. Mostly, she offers hospitality and makes me and others feel welcome by remembering our names. Generally, she supports writers by sponsoring readings by them at her bookshop and encourages artists by displaying their work, even offering their handcrafted cards for sale. She also endorses local musicians by hiring them to play for First Friday events, when people wander from gallery to gallery enjoying new art and music with some wine and snacks. Recently, Leslie touched me by bringing to my apartment a book I had ordered for my sister's birthday. The book had been delayed, and I feared it would be late. I was quite surprised when Leslie offered to send it for me or to bring it by so I could mail it myself with some others in a priority mailbox. I was flabbergasted that she would take so much trouble. When she left, I found a bag of special chocolates along with the book she brought. What a way to say she values me as her customer.

Equally touching was a morning spent at Metro Gallery with Dean Settle. I had stopped to buy a special birthday card for my sister, and before I knew it, I was given a private showing of the Russian painter Ludmila Kuznetsova's work. While discussing her enchanting paintings, several of his cronies showed up, and we all had a great time talking. A watchful host, Dean offered me coffee or water, as his salon continued in conversation. When I admired a small pencil drawing, he explained that it was made by a severely injured veteran living nearby. I was touched by the haunting quality of the work as well as Dean's story about him. I know I'll return at some point to buy one of the small black and white prints. As I sat there, I noticed some interesting books on his bookcase. He said people deposited them with him to sell. I took two, paying $1.00 each and then returning them later. I also noticed one by Stacy Abrams that I hadn't been able to get from the library, so I knew which book I'd get on my next trip. My other reason for going to his shop was to inquire about a brass rubbing that my friend Elaine had given him to sell. She was moving and no longer wanted it. I adored it because it reminded me of living in England in the late 1960s when I took friends and relatives to visit Winchester and Salisbury Cathedrals. When I mentioned my interest, one of Dean's helpers went to the nearby gallery where it was on display and brought it back so I could examine it more closely. He offered to let me buy it in two payments, and that was helpful. It didn't push up my credit card debt too much for that month. He's also taken some oil paintings of mine on consignment to sell. I've had them two decades and would like to buy some new ones with the money from their sale. Since writing this, Dean has retired, but his replacement is equally helpful.

The third downtown executive I'd like to mention is not one I know personally but one I admire for his work in Poland helping Ukrainian refugees. Scott Glenn owns Executive Travel on

O Street and must have a heart of gold. When he heard of the plight of Ukrainian refugees, he went to Warsaw and personally paid for fifty hotel rooms for these and subsequent refugees. Others in Lincoln have also contributed to this fund. Leslie Huerta told me he had contacted her, asking for book titles for young adults that he can buy for youngsters there. Many aren't in school and need some books to read and toys to play with. So, he's obviously a sensitive man trying to help in a tragic situation. Fortunately, the *Lincoln Journal Star* has featured stories about Mr. Glenn and his good work, so many have found out about his heartfelt efforts. He has inspired others to do likewise, and now doctors, nurses, and helpers from Lincoln are in Poland caring for Ukrainian refugees. Ah, the expanding ripples of good deeds!

Limitations and Invisibility

Several years ago, my sister, who is an art therapist and suffers from asthma, told me, "We all have limitations." I was surprised by this statement. But I've slowly seen the wisdom of it. As I age, I have more limitations. I find myself saying more often "Things I used to do ..." After moving to Eastmont, I find others who also experience various limitations, and this forms a bond between us. No one is lamenting too much what "used to be."

This morning as I tried to solve a technology problem, I was reminded of my computer limitations. I could get so far on my smartphone, and then I couldn't complete the task of ordering my mother's death certificate in El Paso, Texas, to send to the lawyer of my brother's estate. Three people who are often available to help me with these problems were not around that morning. I had to admit I might have to wait until Monday to get some help. Not the end of the world, but I was disappointed and angry at myself for my limitations. So, I cried. It was a relief to cry. Then I could see I was being impatient with myself. I prayed about these limitations and visualized laying them at the foot of the cross of Jesus. I admitted I could do no more and asked Jesus to take this burden from me. Then I fell quiet and realized that this experience could be part of my essay. We all confront new or increasing limitations as we age.

Sometimes our limitations are because of our lack of computer skills; sometimes they are caused by increasing health problems (in my case MAC and lack of stamina, which limit my walks); sometimes it's the illness of our friends and their increasing limitations that saddens us. At other times it's memory issues, such as inability to quickly remember names or foreign phrases; a decline in self-image—more gray hair, wrinkles, weight gain, hunching over while walking, and so forth. Everyone has his or her own list or set of limitations, and they grow. It can be unnerving.

Yet, we are all more than our limitations. We are children of God, and God loves us. As older members of society, we may occasionally feel "invisible" or unimportant compared to our former status. Maybe we used to be someone's spouse, sister, or brother, but they have died and we feel diminished. Maybe we used to be a teacher, professor, secretary, or executive with all the self-definition and status that entailed. Maybe we used to have an important role as parent, but now our children are grown. Any of these events can increase our sense of worthlessness. Maybe we used to have leading roles in the stage of our world, but now we're background players. This doesn't feel so good. Sometimes we feel diminished and disregarded. But we adjust and accommodate.

So, it's good to know that God still has plans for us whatever our age, and that God is with us as we experience new limitations. God still equips us for service. Sometimes it's giving others a ride to the doctor or to church. Sometimes it's praying for others. Sometimes it's being a friend and listening. Sometimes it's writing devotions for our church to lift others up. Sometimes it's visiting the sick and infirm. Or it may be taking the time to write an encouraging email or text message to a friend. It can be tutoring someone in English. Sometimes it's making dinner for a friend or inviting friends for tea. Or writing a friend a letter or calling them on the phone, sending an email or a text message. The list is endless and unique to each of us.

An antidote to disillusionment can be found in Carol Christ's book *Diving Deep and Surfacing: Women Writers on Spiritual Quest*. Her essay on Ntozake Shange's choreopoem "for colored girls who have considered suicide/when the rainbow is enuf" is about some of the self-loathing black women feel living in white culture. They often feel discounted for being women, that is, inferior to all men, and for being black. Christ articulates the various characters' suffering and notes one who declares: "i have found god in myself and i loved her, i loved her intensely."

As we age, we continually encounter various existential crises—we're no longer fleet of foot, quick to remember names and words, high energy, youthful looking, quite so able to solve our problems, including technology troubles. This is where spirituality comes to our aid. We can tell God, Jesus, the Holy Spirit, the spirit that moves us, a friend, or even our dog or favorite tree about our deficiencies. Our Higher Power already knows and loves us just as we are. This knowledge can then help us love and accept ourselves. As a friend used to tell me: "We don't have to be perfect to have someone love us." We may not love ourselves as fiercely as Shange's character does, but we can learn to love and accept ourselves. This can be a recurring experience if we are impatient with ourselves and expect perfection, as I often do. My friend Steve Blum recently suggested settling for feeling and being "good enough" instead of seeking perfection. Great suggestion.

If we're really blessed, we can move on to loving "god" within ourselves and understand the saying that we are all icons, that is, representatives of the Holy to others. This is humbling and energizing at the same time. Maybe this is some of what the second part of the quotation from Corinthians means, that though our bodies are going the way of all flesh, our spirits are being renewed day by day as we let God love us back into shape and refresh us.

In her essay on Shange's work, Christ observes that when the characters in the poem lay hands on each other, they experience healing. The laying on of hands affirms her position in a community and the universe, and suggests she is not alone, that others support her. The laying on of hands in a community of women celebrates the power of sisterhood and sharing as one of the keys to a woman's moving through the experience of nothingness (Christ, *Diving Deep and Surfacing*, p. 116).

This experience can also happen in church during the service of healing when the priest and others lay hands on a sick person by serving as a channel of God's love and healing. It can also happen in church during the peace when people recognize, signal, and accept each other. One of the reasons I was drawn to the Ministry of St. Luke was the laying on of hands during the healing service as well as the hugs of others during the passing of the peace. Sometimes when we can't make the existential leap to love ourselves fiercely, our friends help us by laying their hands on us or hugging us.

Beyond Limitations

Some further thoughts on limitations came to me a few days ago. I decided that aging is not just about grieving our lost abilities and accepting the new order. Not just about anger, bargaining with God, and adjusting, or readjusting, to our limitations. Life is also about enjoying a concert or a new book or painting or being with new and old friends. As Chaucer's Wife of Bath says of old age, the bloom has gone, but she will still be "right merry." What a great attitude.

If we keep engaging with what life offers—whether new programs at church, babysitting grandchildren, or going shopping, life is good. Maybe it's learning to coexist with illness or the death of a spouse or good friend. It's as Psalm 30:15 says: "Weeping may last the night, but joy comes in the morning." Each day we get a new morning and a new day of life to live, however we do it. As Martin Luther reportedly said: "Love God and sin boldly." So, let us live life to the fullest—whatever that is each day.

Maybe we're depressed or anxious. It's OK. These feelings won't kill us. They may make us miserable, but they won't kill us unless we catastrophize them. In old age, we probably know where to go and whom to ask for help if we're really depressed and down. Chances are we've dealt with these dark feelings before. Sometimes therapy helps, sometimes sunshine, sometimes vitamins, sometimes our friends, a good cry, a lament, a good movie, book, or work of some kind. Maybe it's learning to be grateful for what we have, not for what we don't have—our old selves, our old energy. What we have now is good enough. We can make the existential statement that who we are is good enough. What a relief!

It may also be comforting to spend some time in prayer and meditation. One avenue to prayer for me is an icon. It serves as a doorway to the Holy. I often admire Rublev's *The Trinity* and find great consolation in gazing at it. I also find solace in *Our Lady of Vladimir*. In this icon, Mary appears sad and mournful as she holds Jesus. When I gaze on it, I realize that my suffering or discomfort is pretty minor. But it's helpful knowing even people as holy as Mary and Jesus felt pain and suffering. It helps me accept my human condition.

Caregiving

A duty that sometimes falls our way as we age is caregiving. While I did a two-year stint of this for my mother in the 1990s when I was in my fifties, nothing prepared me for helping my brother as his night nurse for a few months before he died when I was in my early eighties. We had many good times together, both my mother and I, and my brother and I. With my mom, I heard her reminisce about her youth, which I'd never heard her speak about before. So this was precious. With my brother, he didn't live over old times so much as enjoy reading some of the same mysteries that I did, that is, those by John Grisham, Jacqueline Winspear, and others. We also enjoyed watching the same movies on Turner Classic Movies and *Antiques Roadshow* on PBS. He even got Netflix so we could watch some comedies. Our sense of humor was the same, and we immensely enjoyed two series: Jane Fonda and Lily Tomlin in *Grace and Frankie* and another called *Hart of Dixie* about a northern doctor living in a southern town. Both entertained us in the evenings.

Lately, I served as a caregiver to my friend Elaine Kruse, who's been experiencing agonizing back pain. I wasn't used to this. My mother suffered from Parkinson's and dementia, but she wasn't in terrible pain. My brother, who suffered from twenty-seven different ailments, was in pain, but he had a fentanyl patch and morphine to cope with it. He didn't seem to experience the agonizing pain that plagues my friend Elaine so much. My brother took two morphine pills during the day, and I gave him liquid morphine at night. His pain slowly increased, and the dosage of morphine increased from once a night to every hour. In addition to giving him the morphine, it helped him if I washed his torso and applied fresh cream periodically. Again, this increased from once a night to several times per night. I also had to empty his catheter bag several times per night. It wasn't that this was hard work, but the slow decline of my brother's health and the lack of sleep wore me down. Sometimes I just felt wrung out. Then it was that friends from Lincoln, either Elly Hart, Mary Lutz, or my Sunday afternoon prayer group, called and restored me.

Nature also helped. Once a day, about 11:00, I walked to the pool at his apartment complex. Just seeing the water and the trees and receiving a friendly "hello" from one of my brother's neighbors also restored my soul. One night, there was a super moon, a "blue moon," and it was stupendous. Amazing! I encouraged my brother to walk outside to see it. It was a terrible chore at that time for him to walk with his walker, but he did and was equally impressed. He talked about it for two days, as I recall.

Now, my friend Elaine has been in terrible pain, and I can't do much to help her. I can just sit with her and be present. Eventually, she received some medication and back procedures to help alleviate her pain. So she's managing OK.

At Eastmont and at church, I have seen several couples with one spouse acting as caregiver for the other. I sympathize with both and put them both on my prayer list. It's hard for the sick one but hard on the caregiver too, since he or she is also aging and lacking energy. This is probably one of the hardest parts of aging; having loved ones suffer is hard to see and process.

Chapter VI

Comfort for Our Heart in Literature

Comfort comes to us in many ways. It may come from the Jewish and Christian Bibles, the Koran, or devotionals. One friend, Brenda Goodman, shared that her favorite scriptures were "Lo, I will never leave you, nor forsake you" (Hebrews 13:5) and "Lo, I am with you always, even unto the end of the age" (Matthew 28:20). An interesting take on this I once read was about a Chinese man named Lo, and he thought this scripture was addressed to him personally. After reading this, I put my own name in place of Lo, so that it reads, "Marcelline, I am with you always." This makes this verse extremely comforting. Try it with your name!

A further source of comfort in aging and dying can be found in secular literature. There may be an entire canon of literature on this topic; I'm not sure. However, I have recently found several interesting sources: short stories by Willa Cather, Ann Patchett's essays *These Precious Days*, and Nina Totenberg's memoir of Ruth Bader Ginsburg called *Dinners with Ruth*. Just as it takes a village to raise a child, it may take a village of friends to help me write this treatise. When I mentioned to Steve Shively, a Willa Cather scholar who also attends St. Mark's, my being stymied in writing about aging and spirituality, he mentioned a pamphlet he had edited about Cather that I might find helpful. Indeed, that was the case.

He had edited a pamphlet titled "Aging and Dying in Willa Cather's Fiction." The writers in this piece dealt mainly with two short stories, "Old Mrs. Harris" and "Neighbour Rosicky," both published in *Obscure Destinies*. These stories featured older characters who accepted death, especially after reassuring themselves that their loved ones were coping and would be OK after they died. In reassuring themselves about their families, they also reassured the reader. Moreover, their deaths were in the natural order of things. Both characters were old and infirm. Nothing was tragic about their deaths. Indeed, their lives and deaths almost echoed Julian of Norwich's saying "All shall be well, and all shall be well, and all manner of thing shall be well."

In "Neighbour Rosicky," Cather slowly introduces the reader to his situation. We learn that he is sixty-five years old and has heart trouble. This is significant but not ominous. His story unfolds gently. His doctor tells him to take it easy, and he can live a few more good years. Rosicky takes the doctor's warning seriously, and he looks rather tenderly at the graveyard on the way home. He thought the graveyard was a nice one, "snug and homelike, not cramped or mournful." It wasn't isolated, but wagons would go by and in the summer the mowing machine would rattle up to the wire fence. It was near home. "He was awful fond of his home and not anxious to leave it…. It was a comfort to think that he would never have to go farther than the edge of his own hayfield. The snow, falling over his barnyard and the graveyard, seemed to draw things together. They were all old neighbors in the graveyard, most of them friends; there was nothing to feel awkward or embarrassed about" (Cather, "Neighbour Rosicky," p. 19). The snow and peace of winter gave him time to think on his way home in his wagon. It was reassuring to Rosicky that the graveyard was contiguous to his farm, which he loved. He didn't have to go far to be buried. He was also reassured when his daughter-in-law, Polly, took care of him months later when he had a heart attack at their farm. Rosicky then realized that Polly was tender-hearted and had a sweetness he hadn't known before she nursed him. He realized that she and his son would make it through life all right. In the story, Rosicky had time to review his earlier life before he immigrated to the New World. This apparently is something people often do before dying. It's not maudlin in the story. Soon after reminiscing, he died, knowing that his family would survive OK. In the early twentieth century when Cather was writing, sixty-five years was considered old.

The story "Old Mrs. Harris," is not quite as benign as "Neighbour Rosicky," although the pattern is similar. It focuses on an old lady who is in declining health. Instead of helpful children, she has a rather selfish daughter and ne'er-do-well son-in-law. They are not bad people, just self-centered. Her grandsons and housekeeper Mandy as well as her neighbor Mrs. Rosen care deeply about her and help her as she ails. While old Mrs. Harris does not consult a doctor, she had cared for enough sick people to know that she was unwell and her end near. When Mandy wants to call a doctor, old Mrs. Harris protests. She thinks doctors only want people to linger, and she doesn't want to linger and be a burden to her family (p. 142). Like "neighbor Rosicky," old Mrs. Harris has time to recall the old days when she lived in Tennessee in more flourishing conditions. But when her granddaughter, Vicki, is settled to go to university to study, old Mrs. Harris realizes that her family will be all right in their new place. Then she accepts her impending death and dies. (See Willa Cather, "Old Mrs. Harris" in *Obscure Destinies*, pp. 65–155, and the pamphlet *Aging and Dying in Willa Cather's Fiction*, Betty Kort and Steven B. Shively, editors, Willa Cather Pioneer Memorial and Educational Foundation, Red Cloud, Nebraska, 2005, especially the essays by Marjorie Sirridge, "Sharing Life Stories," pp. 4–9; Mary Sirridge, "Obscure Destinies and Moments of Grace," pp. 10–14; and Susan Rosowski et al., "Death and Dying," pp. 16–23.)

Ann Patchett's essay "These Precious Days" is really an ode to a middle-aged woman named Sooki who suffered and died from pancreatic cancer. Sooki's death is sad because she had become a personal friend of Patchett's and was only sixty-six years old. In the early twenty-first century, sixty-six years is not considered old, and her death did not seem in the natural order of things. Interestingly, Patchett had pondered death since her youth. In the introduction to her essays, she tells us that in her late twenties, she worried about dying before she finished her first novel. No one would be able to finish it for her if she were hospitalized or died because she had made no notes. She carried all her characters and plot around in her mind. She thought doing so enabled her characters and plot to experience greater dynamism. Nor was she alone. She had two writer friends who also worried about dying before they finished their novels. One left her a thumb drive so Patchett could finish her work, and the other left Patchett detailed instructions for the end of her work.

I found this surprising since I wasn't thinking much about death in my twenties. Of course, I worried that I might not face death bravely since this was the time of existentialism, but it wasn't related to writing my thesis in Russian history in the 1960s or my dissertation in the 1980s. I heard tales of others who kept their research materials in a refrigerator in case of a fire. Apparently, fridges do not burn, and their research would be safe. What did frighten me in my twenties was reading Leo Tolstoy's story "The Death of Ivan Ilych." I found it terrifying—as scary as Edgar Allan Poe's "The Tell-Tale Heart." I wondered how Tolstoy could write about death so convincingly. However, as a young wife, mother, and graduate student in the 1960s, I didn't ponder death and dying very much. Moreover, my son, husband, and I were remarkably healthy, so illness did not make me aware of death until my seventies. Rereading Tolstoy's story recently, it struck me as less about Ivan Ilych's death and more about Tolstoy's critique of the hypocrisy in upperclass Russian society. His character Ivan had a hard time coming to grips with his impending death and resented his doctors, family, and friends' pretense that he would recover. Ivan accepted the ministrations of his peasant servant, Gerasim, who understood Ivan's impending doom and willingly served and pitied him. Ivan wanted others to pity and comfort him. In the end, only his son wept and comforted him. Shortly before his death, Ivan participated in the last rites of the Russian Orthodox Church and was comforted by confession and communion. So, though he struggled with loneliness in the months before he died, since everyone avoided discussing his impending death, he experienced resignation and peace at the end. (See Leo Tolstoy, *The Death of Ivan Ilych and Other Stories*, translated by Aylmer Maude and J. D. Duff, New York: Signet Classic, 2003.)

Tolstoy's story is not a comforting tale in the sense of Cather's "Neighbour Rosicky," "Old Mrs. Harris," or her novel *Death Comes for the Archbishop*. At times Ivan's colleagues are crass. One says and feels, "Well, he's dead but I'm alive!" (p. 95). Indeed, his colleagues in the Ministry of Justice mainly discuss their possible advancement when Ivan dies (p. 94). Although one long-term friend named Peter briefly wondered if Ivan could die, maybe he would too, but he soon banished the thought from his mind, thinking death was a natural accident for Ivan but not for himself. Indeed, Ivan was only forty-five when he died. He wasn't an old man, and his death was not in the natural order of things, making it harder for him and others to accept (p. 100).

Patchett also wrote about death in "What the American Academy of Arts and Letters Taught Me about Death." In that essay, Patchett explains that the academy has only 250 members. New ones are added only upon the death of current ones. In looking at an array of the members' pictures, Patchett noted who had died and who was still living. All together, it was a sobering experience being inducted into the academy. It was a sobering essay, but it wasn't macabre.

Likewise, her essay on Sooki was not morbid but an ode to her unusual friend (pp. 230–296). Patchett's writing was comforting because Sooki faced her cancer treatment and impending death bravely. Patchett met Sooki through the actor Tom Hanks. Hanks had written a book called *Uncommon Type*, and Patchett had reviewed it favorably. As a result, she was asked to do a presentation with him. It was through Hanks that Patchett met Sooki, who was his personal assistant. Later it was Sooki who arranged for Hanks to read the audio edition of Patchett's novel *The Dutch House*. As a result, Patchett and Sooki became email friends. A year after their meeting, Sooki told Patchett that she was having treatment for pancreatic cancer and needed to find a clinical trial for further treatment. Since Patchett's husband, Karl, was a doctor, Ann asked him about Sooki's situation. Karl told Sooki to send him her medical file. He shared it with the oncologists at the hospital where he worked, and it turned out that they could include her in their clinical trials right away, whereas her hospital in Los Angeles could not include her for several months, and delay was life-threatening.

Being a gracious southerner, Patchett picked Sooki up at the airport and offered her hospitality during her stay in Nashville. At first Sooki demurred, saying her husband would soon be coming to join her. Patchett insisted, and she and Sooki became close friends, sharing cooking and yoga. Sooki was an ideal guest. Unobtrusive, she had prodigious energy and walked almost two miles to the clinic for treatment and home again on Wednesdays. Sooki also painted energetically, including the charming picture of Patchett's dog Sparky, which appears on the cover of her book *These Precious Days*. Sooki epitomized the scripture that while the body was going the way of all flesh (the cancer eating away at her body), her spirit and energy were being renewed by the creative spirit.

At one point, Sooki tells Ann that at home she had become impatient and angry, and she didn't like herself or her life very much. At Ann and Karl's, Sooki felt like she was a better person. She wasn't just her illness. She was an artist. The fact that her hosts wanted her there, that they loved her, that they believed in her made her believe in herself. Midway through her stay, she didn't want to leave and return to California, where her husband and family were (pp. 282–283).

Sooki tells Patchett that she felt energized in Nashville because she and Karl accepted her illness. She liked herself more. At home in California she felt depleted because after some initial mistakes in her treatment, she felt she had to monitor the cancer technicians and remain hypervigilant. This was a burden that drained her energy. In contrast, she trusted Karl and the doctors in Nashville. She felt protected (p. 292). In an experiment, Sooki and Ann decide to take some special mushrooms that doctors had found helped cancer patients suffering from depression and anxiety. Sooki had a very good experience and realized how much her husband and family loved her. After this she was ready to return home and resume her life there, while taking part in clinical trials in Los Angeles. After the mushrooms, Sooki could even appreciate the cancer since it had drawn her to Nashville and to her special friendship with Ann and Karl. Living with them was worth everything (pp. 288–289). Sooki and Ann brought out the best in each other, becoming their complete selves. It had been a golden time.

Writing after Sooki left, Ann realized that Sooki's visit and the quiet of COVID had given her a sense of order and of God, the God of the Catholic sister Nena, the God of her childhood, and the sense that life is Providential (p. 278). Writing in an epilogue about Sooki's last days, Patchett is not maudlin. She's rather matter of fact in describing their last times together in California. As her husband, Karl, had told her, people die from cancer of the pancreas, and Sooki did. Sooki's illness and resilience show the reader that although death comes for us all, life before death is what matters. She showed how we remain artists of our lives until death.

More comforting than Tolstoy's tale about Ivan Ilych are parts of Feodor Dostoevsky's novel *The Brothers Karamazov*. While the novel teems with stories of the human condition, even debauchery and degeneration in the characters of the father Fyodor Karamazov and in son Dmitri Karamazov, Dostoevsky also depicts two loving characters, Father Zosima and Alyosha Karamazov. Both accept others, never being dismissive or scolding. Their kindliness makes people seek them out for confession and advice. Scores of peasants, townspeople, and young monks flocked to Father Zosima to express their doubts, sins, and sufferings and to seek counsel. Father Zosima is gentle but firm. To a woman frightened of not attaining the afterlife, he encourages her to love actively. He explains that "love in action is a harsh and dreadful thing compared to love in dreams." "Love in dreams is greedy for immediate action ... for approval and applause." "Love in action is labor and fortitude." He advises that learning to truly love her neighbor, she would learn to grow in faith. (See Fyodor Dostoyevsky, *The Brothers Karamazov*, translated by Constance Garnett, New York: The Modern Library, 1937, pp. 55–57.) These words by Father Zosima also influenced the American social worker Dorothy Day, and she quotes the words of love being a harsh and dreadful thing in her book *The Long Loneliness*. Dostoevsky describes Father Zosima's uplifting speech regarding his approaching death. He tells his disciples about his life and how he blesses the sunrise each day but loves even more the sunset, "its long slanting rays and the soft tender gentle memories that come with them, the dear images from the whole of my long happy life—and over all the Divine Truth, softening, reconciling, forgiving! My life is ending, I know that well, but every day that is left me I feel how my earthly life is in touch with a new infinite, unknown rapture, my mind glowing and my heart weeping with joy" (Dostoyevsky, p. 304). Father Zosima encourages us to love all creation—every grain of sand, all plants, animals, and children (Dostoyevsky, p. 334). Zosima declares: "Much on earth is hidden from us, but to make up for that we have been given a precious mystic sense of our living bond with the other world, with the higher heavenly world, and the roots of our thoughts and feelings are not here but in other worlds. That is why the philosophers say that we cannot apprehend the reality of things on earth" (Dostoyevsky, p. 336). Finally, we find redemption in the novel. Toward the end, Dmitri Karamazov confesses that in prison he has found God and himself. Even though he is not guilty of his father's murder, he doesn't mind going to Siberia and suffering in katorga (hard labor) there (Dostoyevsky, pp. 627–628). Likewise, the young boys who had tormented one of their classmates are drawn together at his dying, and Alyosha urges them to remember their good memories and fondness of him and themselves. He assures them this good memory of their childhood will help sustain them in the future (Dostoyevsky, pp. 819–822).

A modern Russian writer who offers consolation about life's difficulties and death is I. Grekova, a trained mathematician. Her novel *The Ship of Widows* describes death in Moscow during World War II. Rereading it recently, I was struck by its comfort. I had forgotten that the "ship of widows" refers to Russian women during World War II who lived on the same floor of an apartment building in Moscow. Fate had drawn them together, and they constituted a surrogate family, alternately fighting with and caring for each other.

While we can belong to surrogate families of friends at anytime in our lives, we seem to depend on our surrogate family more as we age and as our own family members die, fall ill, or move away. This makes us cultivate others in close relationships, much as our brothers and sisters or parents supported us earlier. In the US, the distances and job changes of children and others may limit "real time" with our blood relations. As a result, we may adopt others as our surrogate children, parents, aunts and uncles, or brothers and sisters. While we sometimes base our surrogate families on friends of similar education and social status, sometimes like the ship of widows, we form them on the basis of proximity. This happens when we live in apartment houses and come to know and depend on our neighbors there.

I first observed this pattern of surrogate families among Russian women prisoners who were confined to the Gulag in Siberia in the 1930s. I hadn't known the term "surrogate family" when writing about these women in the 1980s and 1990s. However, at a roundtable discussion at Radford University where I taught in 1999–2000, I heard that it was common for prisoners in the United States to form surrogate families for support while in jail or prison. I had also read an article about female Holocaust survivors forming such groups during World War II. Sharing food and caring for each other helped some Jewish prisoners survive. The same was true of the women in the Gulag. In her novel, Grekova shows how the widows cared for each other, shared food and goods with each other, and tenderly cared for each other during World War II. Her novel comforts us in old age as many of us become widowed and bereft of kin.

Grekova's novel also comforts us when she shows how a slow debilitating death can be a release, for friends and relatives alike. This happens to her character Anfisa, who worked her fingers to the bone for her young son Vadim. She held two jobs, involving hard physical labor. She didn't begrudge her son anything. Only when he went to work in faraway Siberia did she feel rejected and used. Eventually, she suffered a series of strokes, which left her debilitated. Sadly, Vadim recognized his shabby treatment of his mother only at the end of her life. He tried to redeem himself by tending his mother in her last illness, but she was unable to communicate or appreciate his devotion, and his work was almost in vain. So, in this case, Anfisa's death became a relief to everyone in the building's surrogate family. Sometimes something similar happens in our own families when a beloved member loses the ability to communicate or appreciate our ministrations on their behalf. Then we too feel a sense of relief at their death. (See I. Grekova, *The Ship of Widows*, translated by Cathy Porter, Evanston, IL: Northwestern University Press, 1994. Also, see Marcelline Hutton, "Surrogate Families of Soviet Female Pure Victims in the 1930s," paper given at Radford University, spring 2000; this paper explored how women in the Gulag often bonded into small groups or surrogate families on the basis of education, social, political, religious, and even criminal allegiances.)

Nina Totenberg's memoir of Ruth Bader Ginsburg included years of vital friendship as well as an account of Ruth's decline and death. Like Ann Patchett's paen of praise to her friend Sooki, Nina Totenberg's friendship with Ruth was a testament to a woman of courage, strength, and grace. It offered great consolation and was not maudlin. As the book jacket declares, it is a memoir of the power of friendship and as such is not tragic.

Two additional books I'd like to suggest as sources of comfort are by centenarians Sadie and Bessie Delany, who wrote their biographies with the help of a ghost writer, Amy Hill Hearth. Both sisters were born in the late nineteenth century, into the home of a black Episcopal bishop in Raleigh, North Carolina. Their first book, *Having Our Say*, written in the early 1990s when both sisters had turned one hundred, gives their recipe for a good, long life. For them it consisted of doing one's duty to one's profession (Sadie was a teacher and Bessie a dentist), to one's extended family (they had eight siblings and countless nieces and nephews), and to one's community. Neither one complained of life's difficulties, despite growing up black in the Jim Crow South as well as during segregation in New York City around the time of World War I until the 1990s. They tell what it was like but don't dwell on their difficulties. Despite knowing famous writers of the Harlem Renaissance, like Langston Hughes and others, they did not define themselves as hobnobbing with the well-to-do and famous but emphasized their good deeds to their family and community. Their recipe for a long life seemed to involve living a simple, frugal life by eating wisely and well from their own garden and avoiding alcohol and the distractions of a telephone. In her book *On My Own at 107*, written after the death of her sister Bessie, Sadie discusses her difficulty being on her own after having lived with her sister for 104 years. Yet, she seems to suffer through it, goes on with the life God has given her, and doesn't mope about. While Sadie doesn't think she can choreograph her death, as her sister Bessie had wished, she does pray to die with dignity and not end life on a low note, a hope most of us share. (See *Having Our Say: The Delany Sisters' First 100 Years*, Sarah L. Delany and Dr. A. Elizabeth Delany with Amy Hill Hearth, New York: Kodansha International, 1993, and Sadie Delany, *On My Own*, especially p. 69.)

All these writings comfort us in our aging. They help us realize when we remain open to the Spirit we are renewed and need not fear loss, aging, abandonment, or being forgotten. Indeed, if we let the Spirit renew us, we can engage in God's new creation of the present, whatever that is. Readers have their own list of comforting literature, I'm sure. My sister recently reminded me of Marilynne Robinson's book *Gilead*. I had read it several years ago and forgotten about it. It's a fantastic, comforting book about the aging of a Presbyterian minister in a small Iowa town.

Chapter VII

Comfort for Our Heart in Music

Just as I am not a trained literary critic, I am also not a trained music critic. However, I know from life experience that music can be a great comfort to us at any time, including in old age. As I've been pondering which pieces of music speak most to me, I've remembered a few famous ones: Bach's "Jesu, Joy of Man's Desiring," Passacaglia and Fugue in C Minor, and the *Brandenburg Concertos*; Sibelius's *Finlandia*; Haydn's *Creation*; most of Mozart; and Tchaikovsky, especially "Andante cantabile" from String Quartet No. 1 in D Major. Indeed, I had an odd experience with Tchaikovsky's *The Nutcracker* a few years ago. It was at an organ concert at St. Paul United Methodist Church, and the organist played some of the dances from *The Nutcracker* that had been arranged for the organ. As I listened to one of the dances, I felt as though the notes were dancing in my lungs and healing them. It was a peculiar and wonderful experience. I've never felt anything quite like it again. Of course with COVID and cautionary living, I haven't been able to go to many concerts lately, so I haven't been able to explore many musical presentations. I've been to some that were superb entertainment, but none that felt like that particular healing experience. I checked out the Tchaikovsky CD from the library to see if the recording offered the same experience. I also heard some recordings during the Christmas season but wasn't able to repeat the event.

Perhaps it's live music that has the greatest impact on my body. I've been pondering this question.

Since writing this section, I have decided that African American spirituals have also had an enormous influence on me and on our culture. Learning some of these in my junior high music class, I had no idea they would remain embedded in my mind and soul and comfort me as they do. Periodically I look up the lyrics of "There Is a Balm in Gilead" to sing all the words. Others like "Swing Low, Sweet Chariot" are well known in American society. Lately, I've heard myself singing another spiritual: "I'm coming, I'm coming, for my head is bending low. I hear those gentle voices calling, 'Old Black Joe.'" I have found myself singing this when I'm going to meet someone, and I'm walking so slowly down the halls of Eastmont. It just pops out of my mouth. When we're feeling low, "Nobody Knows the Trouble I've Seen" also comforts us.

I did ask some friends over the age of seventy-five about their favorite music, and here are some of their responses. Elly Hart: big band and swing-era jazz and cool jazz, concertos with full orchestras, most classical music, and especially Chopin's piano works. Michael Johnson: big band, bluegrass, Mozart's overture to "The Magic Flute," and the hymn "Now the Day Is Over." Brenda Goodman: Brahms's *A German Requiem*, the hymn "What a Friend We Have in Jesus," and the spiritual "A Quiet Time" by Redd Harper. Elaine Kruse: opera especially, including *La Boheme*, as well as Verdi's *Requiem*, Handel's *Messiah*, and music by Mozart, Chopin, Beethoven, and Benjamin Britten. Corlee Pralle: "Kiss an Angel Good Mornin'," some country western, rock and roll, Elvis Presley, and some opera. My German-American friend Helmi Mays indicated some unusual choices: yoga/zen wordless, rhythmic music and also Philip Glass, John Cage, John Taverner, and Gustav Mahler. Other comforting composers and songs friends have mentioned include Debussy; hymns like "Amazing Grace," "How Great Thou Art," "Because He Lives," and "We Are Standing on Holy Ground"; and Handel's "I Know My Redeemer Liveth."

Two unusual responses to the question of comforting music have come from friends whose husbands liked jazz and brass. One said that her husband planned for jazz musicians to play at his funeral, and she wanted the same. I understood once I heard a jazz musician play a haunting hymn on clarinet at Eastmont one evening. It was beautiful and moving. Another friend said her husband wanted brass music at his funeral, and she did too. Initially, I found this surprising; now, it seems normal.

Chapter VIII

Other Comforts

Comfort Food

A friend recently suggested that as we age we may seek comfort in TV, books, and food, as other segments of the population do. At Eastmont, I find I enjoy many activities with people here: yoga, a monthly book club, sing-along programs, choir, concerts, lectures, craft classes, knitting together, walking, talking, watching movies on Saturday nights, watching the Husker volleyball or football games on TV in the new bistro, and eating breakfast, lunch, or dinner together. We are free to opt into or out of as many activities as we wish. In the four months I have been at Eastmont, I have observed that almost everyone, from age sixty to one hundred, walks a good deal. Some walk inside, some outside. Some go to exercise classes, some use special exercise machines. Most socialize. Most go to church, or to vespers on Sunday evening, or to chapel on Tuesday or Thursday mornings. So, generally, I find most folks at Eastmont stay in good physical shape with exercise, enjoy social times together, and have a spiritual life. Most are reasonably optimistic. The one exception was a person who identified himself as an atheist, and he was very depressed. After hearing this person's confession one happy hour, I thought to myself that atheism doesn't offer much consolation to older depressed people.

In thinking about comfort foods, I realize that they differ according to person. I like oatmeal for breakfast, soup or sandwich for lunch, tea and cake in the afternoon, and meat, potatoes, and vegetables for supper. At Eastmont, my eating habits have changed. I now have a light breakfast of cooked oatmeal, cranberry juice, coffee, and a sweet and enjoy my main meal at 11:30. Contrary to what I have eaten most of my life, it's usually quite a grand meal. There's a choice of five entrees; six sides of soup, Jell-O, salad, potatoes, and vegetables; and a choice of fresh fruit, cake, ice cream, or sherbet for dessert. There's also a choice of beverages: coffee, tea, lemonade, iced tea, milk, and water. One can have as many drinks as one wishes, and some have four different beverages. I haven't figured out how people can drink milk, coffee, water, and even lemonade at the same meal, but a few do. Most, of course, just have coffee and water. I don't entertain friends for cake and tea very often. Indeed, I have seldom made tea and cake or cookies for myself since moving to Eastmont. There's just too much food at mealtime. Free popcorn along with coffee, tea, or lemonade are available day and night. Often there are cookies to have with one's morning coffee, and some partake of them. What I have come to realize at Eastmont is that it isn't so much the food as having friends and acquaintances to share it with, whether at breakfast, lunch, or dinner. While I really like mashed potatoes with meat for my main meal, it's not a prerequisite. Some friends find comfort in macaroni and cheese, others in popcorn, milkshakes, or pizza. Others mentioned licorice, peanuts, popcorn, Jell-O, pecan rolls, and chocolate. I must say that I find ice cream as well as oatmeal to be comfort foods. Tea, coffee, and wine can be comforting beverages. On Friday evenings and at Sunday dinner, free wine is offered if we want it. Some drink it, but many don't, either because they are taking medicines which prevent them or because they don't care for wine. Often, I'm the only one at my table imbibing. That surprised me.

Intellectual Comfort: Reexamining Old Ideas

While I don't review my life often, aging does provide time to examine old ideas. Reading a devotion in the Methodist *Upper Room* one morning, I was struck by an interpretation of scripture that I realized I had misunderstood for decades. It was 1 Thessalonians 5:16–18: "Rejoice always, pray without ceasing, give thanks in all circumstances; for this is the will of God in Christ Jesus for you."

The writer of the devotion emphasized that the scripture said "in" all circumstances, not "for" all circumstances. I had always misunderstood this scripture, thinking it said "for" instead of "in." I had long felt confounded thinking I should give God thanks for all circumstances even when it didn't feel right. In unpleasant experiences, I often felt inadequate because I didn't feel I could give thanks for the crisis. What seemed clear to me now was that I can give thanks to God for being with me in whatever befalls me, not the crisis itself. This was such a relief. Later, I realized that the crisis sometimes drew me closer to God, my reliance on God, and to God's people around me.

Now, I realize that in old age I have time to reexamine and study scriptures and ideas that have previously confounded me and find clarification. I used to think the book of Lamentations in the Old Testament not worth studying because the title sounded so miserable. Then recently chapter 3, verses 19–26, were the Old Testament lesson appointed for our Sunday reading. I was quite surprised to read about hope in Lamentations; chapter 3, verses 21–23 were deeply moving:

> Then I remember something that fills me with hope.
> The Lord's kindness never fails!
> If he had not been merciful, we would have been destroyed.
> The Lord can always be trusted to show mercy each morning.

How beautiful and consoling these verses are! The Lord's kindness never fails and there's mercy each morning. Wow! I was glad to have an opportunity to reevaluate my earlier dismissive attitude toward that Old Testament book. Indeed, I seem to have greater capacity to deal with sadness and misery, at least reading about it, than I did when I was younger. Then I just wanted to avoid anything smacking of unpleasantness.

Another idea I have had the time to reexamine is body image. As a youth, I had hated my body for being so tall and thin. After I married, I hated my body less but still didn't recognize that many body shapes are attractive. Only in old age with the advent of women's sports and seeing tall, thin women athletes in swimming, running, basketball, and volleyball have I accepted that having a healthy body is probably the most important thing, not just being curvy and sexually alluring. In old age, I can see that it has been a blessing to have had a lean, healthy body most of my life. How seldom we count our blessings!

Redeeming and Expanding Our Time

In terms of time and events, I often find if I ask God to bless even small endeavors, God does. Then each errand or writing session goes better. Sometimes God expands our time from chronos to kairos, or from ordinary time to special opportunity, grace-filled time.

Events one Tuesday in April 2022 serve as an example. I had a lot to do: laundry in the morning, lunch, COVID booster shot in the early afternoon, banking in the Haymarket, and then a trip to the Bryan hospital lab to have blood drawn in the late afternoon. Instead of worrying about having the energy to do all these things, I quietly prayed for Jesus to be with me in each activity. Sure enough, each event was strangely enhanced. In the laundry room, I met the daughter of a woman at Pioneer House. The mother had fallen, and the daughter had come from Texas to care for her—washing her bedding, pillows, and so forth. It was good to catch up on what was happening to a fellow P.H. member and get to know her daughter. It was an unexpected and lovely exchange.

After lunch, I took the trolley to the Pinnacle Bank Arena in the Haymarket. At the bus stop, I noticed two others getting off who were using walkers and seemed less mobile than me. So, I gave a silent prayer of thanks for being able to walk with only a cane. Health Department workers at the vaccine site proved very helpful and kind. Those of us with canes and walkers could get our booster shot on the main floor and didn't have to take the escalator to the second floor. That was a boon.

At First National Bank, across the street from the arena, my favorite banker, Ethan Ostdiek, was available to help me. It's always nice to be greeted by name when I have banking to do. I'd received a check from US Bank for closing my account with them, and it was a relief to be able to cash it and get a roll of quarters to help me do my laundry. Since I was in the Haymarket, I thought I'd get a proper lunch because I'd eaten only a snack before I left. I thought I'd go to a restaurant in the old train station. I couldn't find the entrance, and ended up at the Information Bureau. The woman there was helpful and kind but told me the restaurant didn't serve lunch anymore, only dinner. That was a disappointment, but sitting in a comfortable chair, cooling off, and talking to a pleasant person revived me enough to walk one more block to catch the trolley home and make lunch there.

At home, I had a couple of hours to rest up before going to the lab at the hospital. Since everything went smoothly at the hospital, I just gave thanks again for more grace. Today, I realized one more time that God can redeem our busy days and help us not be frazzled. Sometimes God even provides new, engaging, and helpful people to meet along our way. In looking up a definition of kairos, I found one that meant "opportunity." Perhaps that's what happens in retirement and aging; we have more time and opportunity to do things we'd like to do. Writers like Connie Zweig in her book *The Inner Work of Age* and Kathleen Fischer in *Winter Grace* both emphasize the possibilities and responsibility for personal growth in old age. While Zweig sees this as our duty to become elders and workers for social justice, I think we only need to be open to the process of the Holy Spirit's guiding us into fruitful paths. If not everyone wants to be an elder, that's certainly OK.

An example occurred yesterday when a student who sometimes takes me grocery shopping lingered to talk. At first I was surprised that he was interested in some of the art in my apartment and asked me questions about it. Then he asked me about the wooden statues of my brother holding basketballs. I spoke about my brother, about caring for him in Tucson before his death, and about his death. Then the young student told me about his relationships with his grandmother and grandfather in Mexico and about their deaths. Obviously he was close to these two people and perhaps didn't get a chance to talk about them very often. After he left, I thought I probably should have made him some lunch since we were both hungry. I was just surprised that he lingered so long to talk. At first I felt odd that a young man would want to talk to an older woman like me, but then I realized that he might not talk about those losses to his student friends. Regardless of age, we all like someone to listen to us. I have found the same true of homeless people I have encountered in Ft. Lauderdale, Florida, and Lincoln, Nebraska. They seem to want to talk as much as they want money or food. It's times like these that I am thankful to live at Pioneer House where we have neighbors and friends among the residents. When I feel lonely, I can just go to the lounge to read and sit in a recliner, and soon somebody will stop by to chat. Sometimes it's someone using the elevator or coming in from outside. Sometimes it's someone as lonesome as I just looking for companionship.

Unforeseen Circumstances

Unforeseen circumstances can affect us at any age in life. However, they may have more impact when we're older and less resilient. What I have in mind is the destruction of a large building next door to Pioneer House and the construction of an even bigger one in its place. This has brought dirt, dust, and noise pollution in prodigious amounts. My body might not have minded when I was decades younger, but now that I have bronchiectasis and MAC in my lungs, it affects me more adversely. On top of that construction, we have also had almost nonstop destruction and reconstruction in some of the apartments at Pioneer House by part-time residents who don't live here and hence aren't aware of the pollution their renovations cause for the full-time residents. The combination of dust and dirt within and without damaged my lungs even more. For a third time, I have been diagnosed with MAC, which can be caused by bacteria in dust, dirt, or water. So, after I coughed up some blood in the fall of 2021, my pulmonologist decided I will have to take antibiotics for the rest of my life. What a sentence. All from environmental pollution! Luckily I have access to a good Board of Health here in Lincoln, Nebraska, and I finally called them with my lament. The same day, they sent an inspector to Pioneer House to investigate. The damage had already been done to my lungs and to those of a neighbor who also lives on the third floor, but maybe this visit will help contain some of the dirt and dust on the sixth floor, where deconstruction and reconstruction are occurring, and on other floors in the future.

Writing about this topic a month later, I can report only that while the dust pollution seems less, the noise pollution has gotten worse. So, once again I had to write a letter to the Pioneer House board of directors complaining about the noise. This morning, I took direct action and told the workers that they'd have to stop. They were driving me and others crazy. While their noise had forced some residents to leave the building, I didn't have that option because I was doing my laundry. Moreover, I didn't want the bullies to win. So, once again, another letter of complaint and a visit tonight to the board meeting, where I can present my lament. I tried to think of a form of protest all morning and finally called the owner in my outrage. Of course, he didn't answer, but I left a message. After complaining to several people I met and sending an email to a friend in Poland, I felt heard and could let the episode go. Finally, I thought of praying about the incident and then felt better. Prayer is pretty powerful, even when I am outraged and angry. At eighty-two, I realize it's OK to get angry to protect my health and home.

Sobering Events during COVID

As I was writing up a remembrance of my friend Miriam Gelfand, who had died, my heart was heavy. She had been my Russian language teacher at the University of Iowa in 1962, and she was one of my few friends left in Iowa City with whom I shared memories of the 1960s. I was not surprised but touched when her daughter Julia called to tell me of the upcoming celebration of life for Miriam. Not having a car, I couldn't drive to Iowa City for the ceremony, but Julia indicated I could write a remembrance and she would read it at the celebration of life ceremony. After typing up my remembrance, I realized this is a duty that occurs more frequently as we age. At eighty-two, more friends and relations are dying. So we have more funerals to attend and odes to write. It's an honor and a privilege to do so but a sobering experience too.

Equally sobering is the change in our friends. My good friend Elaine Kruse recently moved into retirement housing. Having been a guest many times at her townhouse in Lincoln, I was sad to witness this change. Sad that Elaine now needed the medical care that such a facility provides and sad because her home represented a haven to me. I had stayed there several times, so it meant the end of one way of life and the transition to a new one. I can still visit Elaine in her new apartment, but it's the end of an era when we were both more active as history professors and retirees. Her townhouse abutted Holmes Lake, and she had a small but beautiful patio and backyard with an impressive vista of large trees and well-mown grass. Friends and I had eaten many delicious meals there and spent time lolling in her comfortable patio chairs enjoying Nature with a capital N. Visits to her townhouse had also provided inspiring walks under magnificent trees. All that had come to an end. Who wants the good times to stop? Of course there will be good times with Elaine in her new place, but they will be different. We will have to build a new history there. No small feat in our eighties. In addition to Elaine's moving into Eastmont, another good friend, Elly Hart, moved into assisted living in Columbus, Nebraska. This is more than a hundred miles from Lincoln, so there is little chance of visiting her. Only once have friends taken me there. Living where meals are provided means that my old routines with them are broken. No longer can I call one of them at breakfast or dinnertime, since they are not available. Before, we could often talk while one or the other of us prepared or was eating breakfast or supper. Communication that used to be frequent and easy no longer is. A friend of mine in Iowa City once remarked that once a friend moved into retirement housing, they disappeared into a black hole, and you never saw them again. That sounded pretty bleak. Yet it has happened with my friend Elly Hart. We seldom call or email anymore, whereas we used to see each other frequently, talk on the phone, or email each other. This hasn't happened to my friend Elaine yet, and I pray it doesn't. Elaine still drives, so she's able to come by for tea or sometimes lunch on Saturdays. I'm glad for this but miss speaking with her daily on the phone as I eat breakfast or dinner. (Since then, I have joined Elaine at Eastmont, and we can see each other almost every day and continue to share the good life.)

One sobering event I was not looking forward to was my own need to move to assisted living when my health failed. So far, I am able to live reasonably independently, even though I have bronchiectasis, MAC, and arthritis that impede my walking. Thus far, I am able to pay my cleaning lady to take me grocery shopping once a week, and that has proven helpful. Likewise, the downtown trolley enables me to get out and about to the public library, Walgreens, Leslie's bookstore, Dean Settle's art gallery, Wendy's, movie theaters, concerts, and my church during the week. The trolley doesn't run on Saturdays or Sundays, though, so I have to hitch a ride to church with friends. No doubt the most sobering event will be when I need hospice care at my apartment or perhaps enter a hospice house at the end of my life. However, that may not be threatening but a relief. As we age, we may find ourselves less fearful of serious illness and more accepting of dying. A gentle realization.

Chapter IX

Upheaval of Moving

One undertaking many of us do as we age is move. Many vacate homes they've occupied for decades. Some change houses for apartments, some relocate to retirement homes, some to nursing homes. A dear friend of mine recently moved just as I was settling into Eastmont. She was a good church friend who moved to a retirement community in Minnesota, where some of her family live. I can't begrudge her moving since she and her husband, Don, had planned this before his death last spring. His death just delayed Susan's move since she then had to deal with the paperwork of his funeral as well as the selling of their house. Still, I miss Susan, who was a stalwart at St. Mark's adult forum and 10:30 church each Sunday. It's just that I will miss her, the way my friends at Pioneer House may miss me.

When I sold my house in El Paso, Texas, in 1999, it was hard but not impossible because I was moving on to a job in Radford, Virginia. Moreover, I was only fifty-some years old, and it didn't affect me so much. Then, I left Radford to teach at a college in Klaipeda, Lithuania, and that was hard too but doable. I was just sixty, and life was still adventurous. When I left Klaipeda, I was almost seventy, and it was wrenching to leave my friends of the past decade. I returned to the US and moved to Pioneer House in Lincoln, Nebraska, where I lived for fourteen years. This was the longest I had lived anywhere in my adult life. Moreover, I was eighty-three by then. Moving at eighty-three was tough. I felt the tug of friendship to folks in Pioneer House but also the beauty of the neighborhood, especially the old oak trees, the manicured lawn, and the scampering squirrels. It was wrenching to say "goodbye" to friends, my neighborhood, and my familiar way of life—riding the trolley downtown when I wanted to go to the library, Walgreens, an art gallery, Francie and Finch bookstore, Wendy's, and other favorite places. Although I was looking forward to moving to Eastmont retirement community, it was hard leaving my light, bright apartment on H Street. I knew I needed more support and socializing, but I hated to admit how true this was. Who wants to admit they're lonesome in American culture?

Psychologically, I had some fears of moving. My old insecurities rose to the surface. What if no one at Eastmont liked me or talked to me at dinner? What if Eastmont became a "black hole" from which I would seldom emerge to see old friends or the downtown again? Financially, I was afraid I might not be able to afford it. It costs $2,800 per month, whereas I paid only $400 per month in fees at Pioneer House. My brother had died and left me some money, but I didn't know how long that would last. After a couple of sleepless nights worrying about this, I called my bank, and their financial advisor came to see me to look over my situation. He assured me that I had enough to live eleven years at Eastmont. That seemed like enough time. I sold my apartment to a couple who lived across the hall from me, and this windfall plus my brother's legacy seemed enough to take care of me. In addition to assuring me about my finances, the financial planner reminded me that we have seasons in our life, and that while my season at Pioneer House was ending, a new one was beginning at Eastmont. That was reassuring, and I felt more confident about moving.

I decided to personally tell all my friends at Pioneer House that I was leaving. I wanted to do it one by one and not have them hear about it secondhand. This was difficult but not as heartrending as I imagined. I had already told my Pioneer House friends Michael and Corlee, so it wasn't so wrenching telling others. Many were supportive and understanding.

It was bittersweet saying goodbye to friends. I decided to have a farewell party and serve root beer floats. Corlee helped me serve the floats to the sixteen people who came, and we had a good time. It felt good to say "goodbye" and not just slink away.

Packing Up

It was physically and mentally more tiring packing and unpacking than I expected. At night, I lay awake pondering what to take, what to donate to the "put and take" downstairs, and what to throw away. It was hard to silence my monkey mind at night. Much to my surprise, my back ached less at these two times than it had previously. It turned out that bending, packing, and unpacking were beneficial exercise. Who would have guessed? It was a great help having Corlee help me pack. She helped me tape boxes, take unwanted things to the basement for "put and take," and dispose of the rubbish in the garbage outside. She and two other friends, Rita and Rayma, also helped me take sixteen bags of books to the public library. Getting rid of books lightened my moving load. Indeed, Corlee and friends who prayed for my move reminded me of how well God provides for us. Still, one Sunday I was so exhausted that I thought I might have a nervous breakdown or a stroke, so I just relaxed all afternoon on my chaise longue, reading instead of packing.

Unpacking and Moving In

While it was emotionally jarring and physically exhausting sorting and packing, the unpacking went more quickly. When I lay awake in bed before the move I tried to think of what and how to pack. After I'd moved, I lay awake and tried to imagine where I would put things. Some items, like my coats and jackets, easily fit in the front closet. Others like my dresses and blouses could hang in my walk-in closet. Bed linens, tablecloths, napkins, scarves, and purses were harder to allocate. But it seemed easier to unpack than to pack. I decided to put winter sweaters and flannel sheets in suitcases in my storage unit, which is on the same floor as my apartment. Likewise, all my suitcases and many pictures I couldn't find space for fit into the storage unit. Within a couple weeks, I had everything put away, and that felt good.

Moving Surprises

Two things about moving surprised me. One, my back hurt less because I was busy moving around all day and evening. Two, I was happy being busy. I sometimes feel depressed, and sometimes it's because I have so little to do besides read books, write, and watch TV. I actually felt happier while packing and unpacking than I had for some time.

The last item I unpacked was my computer. That was a sign, of course, that I had ignored my writing about aging and spirituality for three months. Although I knew I wanted to write about the trials and tribulations of moving, it was easy to avoid doing so. Yet, it felt good to set up my computer, plug it in, and see that it still worked. It's old for a computer, about twelve years old, but it works for entering text for books. I was surprised at how good it felt to read and edit some of this piece. It felt even better to write about moving. I knew it would be easier to write if I gave myself some time to mull over my experiences. When I used to write travel pieces, I waited about two weeks to let my thoughts settle. So I did the same thing this time. Then I was ready to write. Amazing. Like a miracle. As I began to write, I realized that I wasn't the new kid on the block anymore because a host of new people had moved into the new building, Stratford, just a couple weeks after I moved to the Sycamore. So it was interesting to greet newcomers and try to make them feel welcome, as others had done for me.

As I was taking some notes on Morrie Schwartz's book *The Wisdom of Morrie* I kept thinking that his ideas about aging as a process of reflection, integration, and transformation (p. 218) also fit with moving and to some extent traveling too. Moving and traveling also provide time to reflect, to integrate our ideas, imagination, and sense of self into a new coherent whole. There's a sense that new surroundings can give us new perspectives and offer new beginnings. I've experienced this somewhat moving to Eastmont. I have new opportunities to reflect on my past as I unpacked my belongings, especially old pictures of

Upheaval of Moving

my son as a baby, early years of married life, and so forth. It was a very good time to look back at those pictures and reminisce about my past. Now, living at Eastmont and making new friends and acquaintances is also positive. Lately, I've been more motivated to work on my book, and that feels great. It seems easy to tell people here that I'm writing a book on aging and spirituality. I seldom spoke of my work when I lived at Pioneer House, so this is a different and more supportive environment for me. I guess it shows that I am taking myself and my work seriously. It seems easier to do because many people at Eastmont are former teachers, and I feel as if they care about me and my writing. It's especially helpful that I can go to lunch at 11:30, sit down with four or five others, and enjoy a lovely meal that waitresses serve us. I've decided that having lunch breaks up my day, and that feels good. Eating a big meal restores me to return to my unit and work another bit. Also, if I eat lunch, I can eat supper in my apartment and watch PBS news at 6:00. I like the tone of this news best. It seems more balanced than CNN, MSNBC, or FOX. Moreover, the PBS newscasters are old friends I enjoy spending time with. Another reason for eating lunch is that sometimes I feel depressed in the morning, especially when the weather is gloomy. Gray skies sometimes make me feel a sense of impending doom. Going to lunch breaks this mood and cheers me up to return home to read, take notes, write, or type on my project.

So, while moving to Eastmont has been a positive experience, and I like the activities—especially yoga, swimming, attending concerts, and eating meals with other residents—I now realize that part of me felt in a funk about finishing my book. It was easy to fall into the busy life and entertainment that Eastmont offered. Many activities were fun, and I hadn't taken much time for play most of my life, so I may have been making up for lost time. Who knows? Not surprisingly, my old demon procrastination took over, and I fell into reading novels and watching movies on TV instead of sitting down to work on this book a little bit each day. Writing is work. I just wanted to play. Also, I wanted to avoid facing any criticism that finishing my book might bring. I'd faced this dilemma five times before, but it seemed more paralyzing this time. Was aging the answer? I'm not sure. At eighty-four, I think in terms of writing only twenty to thirty minutes a day. I've discovered that it takes me longer to revise fifty pages than it used to. Likewise, I became aware that it is harder to write thank-you notes. It seems easier to just write an email or a text. Maybe all writing is more of an effort than I realized.

It was helpful when I heard a fellow at breakfast complain that it was more difficult for him to write articles now than it had been previously. This struck a chord. I didn't say anything to him, but I pondered his words in my heart. Around this time, two readers of my manuscript told me they liked it. This was reassuring and encouraging. All of a sudden I felt something shift inside me. I felt I could revise my work and that I wanted to revise and finish it. I asked a friend to pray for me to be able to work on the book. That was something I'd never done before. I'd learned to pray before writing, but I had never asked someone else to pray for my writing. This was a vulnerability I had never accepted before. Reaching out for help was something new. Maybe we do the same thing when we die. We let others see how vulnerable we are and let them minister to us.

Loneliness and Depression

The feelings of loneliness and depression sometimes influence our desire to move. I felt pretty lonely and often felt depressed during the gray days of winter and spring. While I've composed a little ditty about gray days that makes me laugh at my depression, I've found that an early lunch with other people also cheers me up and eases the depression. Sometimes working on my book lifts my spirits. Sometimes praying for others and myself helps. Writing in my journal is useful. Reading scriptures and devotions renew my spirit. Reading Psalm 103, especially verse 4 about God redeeming me from the pit of whatever "hard emotion" I may be feeling, helps a lot. Reciting Psalm 23 at night when I'm sleepless is comforting. Thinking of God as my shepherd assuages my fears and concerns, especially the phrases "He restores my soul; He leads me in the paths of righteousness for his name's sake" and "though I walk through the valley of the shadow of death, I will fear no evil; for you are with me; Your rod and Your staff comfort me." Recently, I have discovered a Jewish prayer, "On Retiring for the Night," also as a source of solace. This lovely prayer was given to the members of our adult forum by Steve Blum, who presented a program on Jewish prayers to us one Sunday. Thus, help comes to us from many sources.

Fresh Breezes of Spirituality

In the spring of 2022, St. Mark's parishioner Steve Blum led a study of Julian of Norwich for our adult forum. He's a masterful teacher and former counselor. He apparently first gave this program via Zoom during the height of COVID from a nearby monastery. It seemed appropriate to him because Julian lived during several plagues and the Hundred Years' War in fourteenth-century England. In such dire circumstances, she had visions of God's love, tenderness, and goodness. While she is most famous for her saying that "all shall be well, and all shall be well, and all manner of things shall be well," she had fifteen visions or showings and insights. One I particularly liked is "sin is its own punishment." In retrospect, this seems true. I often convict myself after an unkind word or deed—gossip, envy, sloth. Other of her sayings include "I am the supreme goodness in every kind of thing. I am the one who causes you to love. I am the one who causes you to yearn" and "… as truly as God is our Father, so truly is God our Mother. Our Father wills, our Mother works, and our Master, the Holy Spirit, empowers" (both from chapter 59 in her *Revelations of Divine Love*).

The other night, a friend in our Bible study cited a scripture about being willing to be willing. It stuck in my mind. I decided it applies to writing. If I am willing to sit down to work, something happens. I become engaged and enjoy writing. But sometimes I dread beginning. I'm not willing to begin. But if I think about being willing to be willing, it's easier to start.

Sometimes I lack self-confidence in writing. I think, "Who am I to write on aging and spirituality? I'm not a theologian or doctor. I'm just a lay person." Then I think, "If I'm willing, God will provide the words. God doesn't call the equipped, but equips the called."

I also thought how appropriate this phrase is for aging people. We just have to be willing. We don't have to do great things, just be willing to do some of the simple, kind things that cross our paths daily. It can be making soup with a friend; serving it later to friends; visiting a shut-in on the phone or in person; smiling at those we meet; taking time to send a friend a birthday card or get-well card; giving a ride to someone; or telling God thanks for a good day and a beautiful sunrise or sunset. The list is endless. Good deeds are endless. Even my banker did one for me today, telling me of a special higher interest rate for my savings.

Giving Ourselves a Break

One of the most important things I've learned from Julian is to give myself a break. Growing up in the 1940s and '50s, I somehow imbibed the notion of perfectionism. I have often striven to be perfect or perform perfectly even though I know in my mind this is impossible. Moreover, I have often judged others for not being perfect. Ever since my son chided me, saying "No one is perfect," I felt indicted. I knew in my mind that no one is perfect, but I didn't know it in my heart. I still nursed my childhood belief in perfectionism. It has taken a lot to finally shake that idea. However, reading a long passage from the Gospel of John in Russian for our Pentecost service of May 2023 finally jarred me out of my old idea of perfectionism. Even though I practiced reading the gospel in Russian twice a day for a week, I noticed that I mispronounced two syllables in my reading for Pentecost. Several of the verbs had five syllables with a host of consonants, not easy reading. I was frightened of making a pronunciation error. Before the service, Steve Blum suggested that we tell ourselves not "I did the best I could" but simply "I did well enough." These days, I often find myself saying "I am good enough" or "What I am doing is good enough." Not perfect but good enough. Cutting myself some slack. This prevents me from falling into critical perfectionism and scolding myself and others so much.

Reading the Episcopal *Forward Day by Day* this morning, I noticed the author referred to Peter's continual misunderstandings of Jesus, yet Jesus had abiding love for him (*Forward*, June 9, 2022, p. 42). Reading some of Julian of Norwich's revelations, I had the same experience. She emphasized that we continually miss the mark and make mistakes, yet God still loves us. I'm beginning to accept these ideas as blessings. As the devotion this morning said, "If perfection were possible ... we would have no need of a savior" (ibid.).

So, growing older, I am giving up some of the harshness of perfectionism in favor of cutting myself and others some slack and in favor of forgiveness. I'm beginning to see that to sin and to make mistakes are normal, human, and we can lament, accept God's forgiveness, and go on in peace. As Julian said, we learn to ask for mercy and accept God's forgiveness with humility. It's a good idea to be more humble as we age, since we are bound to err and need help from others.

I read a telling article on aging in yesterday's *Wall Street Journal*. This one was titled "The Hardest Part about Getting Older: Acceptance," by Sherry Mendelson. In her article she discussed her fears about aging and needing help. When she had knee surgery, she found herself needing her husband and daughter to help her. She found this very disconcerting. As a physician and parent, she was used to caring for her daughter and others, not having them help her. She feared her husband of thirty-seven years might leave her if she was too demanding and needy. So aging, illness, and recovery can tap into our fears and lack of self-confidence. It took recuperation to teach her that her husband, daughter, and granddaughter all wanted to be with her, sick or healthy, independent or dependent. Only then could she relax and appreciate their kindness. Only then was she truly grateful for her new knees, her husband, and her family. Interesting how illness and incapacity can teach us a lot about ourselves and help us grow psychologically, socially, and spiritually. (See "The Hardest Part about Getting Older: Acceptance," by Sherry Mendelson, *The Wall Street Journal*, Thursday, November 17, 2022, p. R8.)

Not Aging Ourselves

Reading another devotion the other morning in the Methodist *Upper Room*, I was struck by a sixty-one-year-old woman's lament about her life. She had just finished a degree but hadn't gotten the job she wanted. She was feeling down about being "too old." I was shocked because sixty-one seems young to me. Then I thought, I can't use old age as an excuse anymore. I could see how inappropriate it was for the sixty-one-year-old, and I thought it might not be good for me to excuse or accuse myself because I'm in my eighties. I realized that in both cases, it's not our age but our willingness to respond to life, opportunities, and service that's the secret. God doesn't abandon us at any age, and we don't have to disparage ourselves because of our age. We can be willing to serve, as John Donne put it on his death bed, "in thy way, in thy time, and in thy manner"

(Donne, Meditation V, p. 35). Also, it's good to remember that God called Abraham to leave Canaan and begin a new life when Abraham was in his seventies, and God called Moses in his eighties to lead the Hebrews out of Egypt. So who knows what God may yet call us to do. Recently, I read Genesis 46:3, where God says to Jacob, "Don't be afraid to go to Egypt." The context, of course, is that Jacob's beloved son Joseph is in Egypt, and Jacob wants to see him before he dies. However, Jacob is an old man by the time Joseph's whereabouts are revealed to his brothers and father.

While we can be afraid to do something new at any age, it is especially hard as we age. I've discovered this as I think of moving to a retirement place with more programs than Pioneer House offers. Moving is disruptive. Consulting my bank's financial planner about whether I could afford to live at Eastmont and a real estate agent about selling my apartment was hard to do, but they were but reassuring interviews to have. Daily life and routine are comforting. Why disturb ourselves for new adventure? New friendships? New endeavors? A new abode? The answer seems to be because God continues to call us and speak to us. As I read recently, God doesn't call the qualified; God qualifies those called. What a refreshing thought. We don't have to shun new adventures. God will equip us. So we trust in the Lord to equip us for our journeys, encounters, experiences. It was heartening to read recently of a seventy-six-year-old woman in Florida who tired of watching plays in which old people were the butt of jokes. She decided she could write a play featuring older actors in respectable roles. And she did. Indeed, she was concerned about the defrauding of older people and decided to write a play about scamming. She found that bringing fraudulent practices to light helped defuse the shame associated with falling prey to a scam and helped others avoid becoming the next victim. Her advice included "You should never have to give money to get money" and "If you don't recognize the number, use voice mail to screen your calls." She has written several plays so far, about fall prevention, surrendering car keys, and even dementia. In Florida, a group called SAGES, an all-senior theater group, acted out her plays with wit and humor. (See article by Hannah Critchfield, *Tampa Bay Times*, reprinted in "Theater Helps Older Adults Fight Scams," *Journal Star*, Prime, Performing Arts, October 2022.)

Likewise, an *Upper Room* devotion for November 2, 2022, tells the story of a woman who at seventy-eight began a ministry of sending cards to those being prayed for. She ended up sending twelve thousand cards, and the ministry continued after her death. So, we never know how we might bless others, if we are willing to answer God's call. Seems like we are never too old to serve.

Becca Levy's book *Breaking the Age Code* reminds us to avoid ageism and having negative thoughts about our age. She argues that having positive thoughts of aging can increase our lifespan more than seven years. Some American women discovered during COVID how good it was to accept their age when they stopped dying their hair to disguise the gray. They were happy to spend less time and money in hair salons. I was surprised that it was so empowering for these women to "go natural." I had never had gray hair until my seventies, so I hadn't personally suffered from aging in my fifties, as some of these women had. I had stopped getting perms in my hair in my late seventies and let it be natural. I found this too was liberating. It's a relief to be who we are.

Much to my surprise, I noticed a citation in the *Wall Street Journal* article mentioning that children as young as age three internalize negative stereotypes about aging. English researcher Louise Pendry, at the University of Exeter, noticed that young children often thought old people were incompetent. Levy had noticed the same thing, and after reading it in two different sources, I realized there might be some truth in this observation. Since women are often regarded as less competent than men, this was a double whammy for older women. The article then noted that whereas women employers felt comfortable hiring women with gray hair, men did not. So, there can be an economic price to pay for being authentic and letting one's hair be gray. (See "Gray Hair Is New Power Move for Women in the Workplace," by Rachel Feintzeig, *Wall Street Journal*, Monday, September 26, 2022, p. A11.)

Wanting Others to Be Strong for Us

A trap I have sometimes fallen into is wanting others to be strong for me. When I once complained to my priest in Iowa City about my sister's serious asthma, she said to me, "Why do you need your sister to be strong for you?" I didn't know what to say. I didn't know that I was a dependent personality and liked to depend on others to help me and be strong for me. When they failed me, as my father and husband had, I felt bitter and angry. Even now, when I depend on my friends and they disappoint me by being human, I sometimes feel abandoned and alone. It takes me a while to realize that they are not abandoning me by their actions, but that their needs and actions are theirs, and they are following their agendas, not mine. When I can free myself from feelings of dependency and abandonment, I can see that my friends are not deliberately letting me down. They are simply doing what they need to do. In a way, this brings me to remembering that only God is completely dependable and available. Human beings can't always be available to me, and that's OK. Moreover, just as my friends are a mixture of strength and weakness, so am I. The fact that I have made it into my eighties indicates that I have some strength as well as weakness. Moreover, I now realize that I sometimes disappoint myself and let myself down. Instead of finishing this book or doing revisions, I often watch a movie on Turner Classic Movies in the afternoon, read a mystery, or talk to friends. None of these is wrong, but if I want to make progress, I need discipline. So, I can forgive myself and do twenty minutes of work before watching a movie.

Psychological Aids to Aging

It was when I was in Iowa City in June 2022 that a friend who had served as a hospital chaplain recommended some books about aging. I have read three that are very helpful, and I have mentioned them throughout this book. One is by Connie Zweig, *The Inner Work of Age: Shifting from Role to Soul*; the second is by Becca Levy, *Breaking the Age Code*; and the third by Kathleen Fischer, *Winter Grace: Spirituality and Aging*. Their approaches are slightly different, and their focus different from mine. But I recommend them all very highly for their insights about what individuals can do to grow as they age. Zweig discusses the divine messengers of aging, illness, and death and our responsibility to deal with our shadows to help us grow. She sees our shadow as our inner critic, the doer, provider, victim, inner ageist, and so forth. These are often negative projections we project onto others. But if we make friends with our shadow, we may encounter hidden gifts and talents that may have lain dormant during our busy lives (Zweig, pp. xiv, xv, xix, and 10). Zweig also encourages us to develop our soul to serve our families and communities as elders and work for social justice. After reading Zweig, I wondered if everyone is equipped or desires to deal with their shadow. Not everyone has access to a therapist, and maybe some people prefer to deal with these issues differently. Today, I read a quote by famous therapist Karen Horney, who wrote "Fortunately analysis is not the only way to resolve inner conflicts. Life itself still remains a very effective therapist" (*The Quotable Woman*, Philadelphia: The Running Press, 1991, p. 129). I finally decided that not everyone has to become an elder; some will and some won't. None are failures. I also don't think retirement is just for working to improve ourselves. It's certainly a time to grow, but I think this is an organic process, one we engage in but don't always direct. It's a time to be open to the Spirit and grace. Life is organic, and it develops differently for each of us. We don't have to push the river. At times, Zweig can seem a bit too prescriptive.

I agree with Zweig's goal about confronting our shadows, but I don't think this is a solitary task. Encountering our shadows, becoming elders, and working for social justice may be activities that we can do in community and in an organic way, as part of the flow of life. The spirit that moves us can be a holistic force as well as an individual inward movement that confronts our

Upheaval of Moving

shadows or adopts more positive age beliefs, as Becca Levy suggests in *Breaking the Age Code*.

Levy's book helps make us aware of being ageist in our ideas and suggests ways we can avoid ageist stereotypes, just as we are learning to avoid being sexist and racist. I used to proudly describe myself to others as eighty-some years old. But now I realize I don't have to define myself in terms of age in hopes of getting compliments like, "You don't look eighty." Now, I know I don't have to put myself down with ageist remarks or seek compliments about looking younger. I just don't have to engage in these two behaviors.

Levy also encourages us to redefine our models of older people. She asks us to list adjectives that define older people and decide which are negative and which are positive. She urges us to stick with the positive and develop positive age ideas. When I did this, I remembered a great-grandmother who was the epitome of loving-kindness. Great-grandmother Iselman invited us for Sunday dinner when I was a child. Born in 1868, she was already in her late seventies when I was a child in the 1940s. Her husband had died in 1944, and her youngest daughter, Marjorie, lived at home with her husband and son. So when Grandma Iselman invited our family of five to dinner, she was already cooking for four. So, all together, she cooked dinner for nine people. As far as I remember, it was a happy occasion. It was one of the few times our whole family did something together. I don't remember if my mother took food, she may have, and she probably helped with the cleaning up, but still it was quite an undertaking for my great-grandmother to offer us such fabulous hospitality so many Sundays. I certainly remember her as a kind, white-haired, and gentle person. She was a good model for old age. The surprising thing to me when I looked at some of the family genealogy is that she lived longer than her children. She died at age eighty-nine in 1957, while her children died in their sixties and seventies. Of course, this great-grandmother's father, my great-great-grandfather Frank Letcher, lived to be 101, dying in 1936. Maybe their longevity was in their genes, maybe it was in their kindliness, maybe a combination.

Cooking and offering hospitality as my great-grandmother and mother did are just two ways of feeding others and our own souls. But there are so many others. The spirit that moves us restores us in nature—the trees, animals, and flowers; the restorative power of water; in exercises like tai chi and walking; in studying scripture; hymns; worship; poetry; art; music; handicrafts and hobbies that are creative and awe inspiring; travel; and countless other activities.

While we may have inculcated some negative ideas about God as children or youth, as older adults we have the time to investigate more positive descriptions. Some I found the other night while rereading Psalm 103 include the following phrases about God's love and concern for us. After the invitation to praise the Lord, come the wondrous words to

> Forget not all the Lord's benefits:
> Who forgives all your iniquities;
> Who heals all your diseases;
> Who redeems your life from destruction;
> Who crowns you with loving-kindness and tender mercies;
> Who satisfies your mouth with good things;
> And restores your strength like an eagle's.

Meditating on these verses, I have come to regard them as promises that are consoling. It's comforting to hear that God forgives our iniquities and heals us. God has created us so that minor injuries like cuts and scrapes often heal themselves with some soap, salve, and fresh air. In April 2023, I received a terrific thump on the back of my leg. It created a hematoma the size of my fist, but my leg slowly healed itself. Whenever I asked doctors about it, they just said keep exercising. So I did. There are many natural ways to heal that aren't costly or time consuming. Walking on the Appalachian Trail has healed some PTSD sufferers. Walking generally strengthens our body, mind, and spirits. For more serious ailments, God provides doctors, nurses, and other healers to help us. Of course, we all have to die of something, but if we're blessed we can fall asleep in the arms of Jesus, however that occurs. Some are fortunate to fall asleep in the arms of their spouse, children, doctor, nurse, or friends.

I especially like the verse in Psalm 103 that says the Lord redeems our life from destruction—whatever that is, depression, anger, guilt, grouchiness, suicidal thoughts, financial woes, loss of loved ones, our inner critic, our shadows, whatever besets us, whatever we fear, even death itself. While I've been blessed with financial serenity from adequate Social Security and a small teaching pension, millions of seniors lack adequate financial resources for their golden years. Still, God may bless them in other ways.

The next verse is almost unbelievable: the Lord crowns us with loving-kindness and tender mercies. We may experience these in various ways. Sometimes it's when a friend, spouse, or child loves or forgives us for an unkind word or action.

Sometimes it's when a friend or a child does a kind deed for us. I have friends who give me rides to church and to the doctor, who listen to me and encourage me.

Sometimes it's when a friend shares some sweet potatoes, cake, or pie with me. This counts as loving-kindness. Sometimes it's a kind word from a neighbor. Sometimes it's help from my pharmacist when my prescription runs out before the end of the month, yet he's able to refill it. Sometimes it's the kind deed of a librarian getting a book for me or engaging me in conversation, which brightens my day! Sometimes it's the helpfulness and service of waiters Alex and Jordan at Billy's restaurant, which used to be my neighborhood restaurant. God's loving-kindness seems to know no bounds when we meditate upon it. Sometimes it's a charming email from a friend in Lithuania, Poland, or England. Sometimes it's a long, thoughtful email response from my sister Kathryn that makes me glad I'm alive and that she's my sister. Sometimes it's the weekly phone call from my son Martin. That always cheers me up and makes me feel like the beloved mother I am. In the US we are so blessed with abundance that God satisfies our mouth with good things, and our youth (strength and enthusiasm) is renewed like an eagle's. I used to be surprised, but glad, when people thought I was younger than I am. Now, I feel more like my sense of well-being is restored. I don't have to feel young but grateful to be enthusiastic about life.

Of course the Bible is full of scriptures telling us how good God is, but there's a phrase in James 1:5 that spoke to me last week: "God gives to all generously and ungrudgingly." That really struck me. Sometimes we are generous but grudging. Only God is completely good and merciful.

Upheaval of Moving

It seems there are examples of people aging well all around us. There was an interesting article about William Shatner, a star in *Star Trek* in the 1960s, who is still excited about acting when he is in his nineties. In an interview for the *Wall Street Journal* in September 2022, Shatner said that he's "awed by the wonders of life and the mysteries of the universe" and is still learning as an actor. Moreover, his journey into space in October 2021 changed him. He grieves that we are not taking better care of our tiny planet. He has become more philosophical about life and more thankful for each day. He said in a 2004 album "Live life like you're gonna die / Because you're gonna." Still he notes that he is energized by his acting talent. He thinks he's a better actor now than he's ever been. He's better organized. He quips, "I'm at the tip-top of my game. But my shoulders hurt." (See "William Shatner," by Emily Borrow, *Wall Street Journal*, Review, Saturday/Sunday, September 17–18, 2022, p. C6.)

Some Changing Attitudes and Circumstances of the Aging

It's been gratifying to notice glimmers of change in British and American society toward the elderly. While many elderly struggle to survive economically, some are finding fame and fortune in old age. Indeed, many older people find great purpose in continuing to work, whether it's writing books, performing on stage, making videos, or caring for the aged. There was a fascinating account in the *Wall Street Journal* in December 2022 that recounted the saga of two Brits in their seventies who have hundreds of thousands of followers on TikTok, Instagram, and in the English Midlands who enjoy their music. Indeed

Pete Bowditch and Basil Bellgrove have transformed how some young people perceive older people to be more positive. Known as Pete and Bas, their young fans buy their T-shirts and CDs and enjoy hearing them in person. The duo began singing in public in 2017 and depended on their grandchildren for slang in recording their music. (See "Hip Hop's Breakout Stars ... in Their 70s," *Wall Street Journal*, December 27, 2022.)

Other articles in the *Journal* detail how many older people find meaning and money in caring for the elderly. One man enjoyed taking a senior golfing. Some elderly need the money and work full-time. Others work part-time for luxuries. One article interviewed several people in their eighties who were financially insecure and needed to work for the money, and some who were happy to entertain others by playing games and puzzles with them or by writing letters. Some did the shopping; some did personal care, such as bathing. Employers of home help agencies find workers over fifty very dependable. Another article discusses how much some employers appreciate older workers' reliability and work ethic. (See Claire Ansberry, "More Seniors Are Filling Labor Gaps in Elder Care," *Wall Street Journal*, March 7, 2023, p. A10, and Callum Borchers, "Older Workers Are in Demand When Bosses Want Work Ethic," *Wall Street Journal*, Thursday, April 6, 2023, p. A11.)

Another story reported the work of a 103-year-old doctor named Gladys McGarey, who lives in Scottsdale, Arizona. She rides a three-wheel tricycle and takes 3,800 steps each day. She retired at age eighty-six but kept working unofficially, going to Afghanistan to teach women safer birthing practices. According to her, the secret to continued work is doing what makes "your heart sing." As ninety-nine-year-old financier Charles

Upheaval of Moving

Munger reported, "You don't call it work when you enjoy it." (See "At 103, Work Still Makes Heart Sing," by Clare Ansberry, *Wall Street Journal*, Wednesday, January 3, 2024, p. A11.) So, for some, continued work is a blessing, not a burden.

A year after the story ran about rappers Basil and Pete, another story about a British woman rapper named Joy France emerged. She's not only a rapper but a "battle rapper." Initially, she was horrified to think that label meant rapping about anger and hate, but it turned out to be more diverse than that. As a former teacher, Joy soon realized that just as some of her former students had struggled with depression and mental health issues, battle rap was more about mocking or taunting one's opponent than she had understood. A crowd determines who wins a match. She's good, but her opponents are too. (See "Retiree Takes On Britain's Rap Scene," James Hookway, Manchester, England, in the *Wall Street Journal*, Monday, October 2, 2023, p. A12.)

In the US, changing attitudes and fortunes are sometimes reflected in TV and the media. Ashley Wong writes about changing TV culture in the popular show *The Bachelor*, which featured a retired man of seventy-two, Gerry Turner, and twenty women contestants over sixty. Turner had been widowed for several years, and when he saw a call for senior contestants, his daughters encouraged him to apply. He became the first "Golden Bachelor." I watched the first episode, and as I write, a friend reports that the twenty women contestants in subsequent shows have been reduced to four. Apparently ABC executives had noticed a cultural shift toward celebrating senior citizens. As contestant Turner remarked, people don't give up the desire for romance, love, and new adventures. "You never, never give up on trying to be social and finding someone to spend your life with." (See Ashley Wong, "Nation's New Eligible Bachelor Is a 72-Year-Old Grandpa," *Wall Street Journal*, Thursday, September 18, 2023, pp. A1, A14.)

Watching the wedding of the Golden Bachelor several months later, it was fascinating to see how happy he and his bride were. It seems that their courtship made the TV show very popular with an older audience. Hopefully, it will help younger folks reconsider what aging is or can be like.

While this article does not indicate how much money Turner made doing this show, a later article does indicate that some retirees who make YouTube and TikTok videos are earning six-figures from various sponsors. My favorite characters in the report are a mother, Lynn Davis, age sixty-seven, who helped her unemployed son, Tim Davis, make videos during COVID in 2020, and she ended up famous. She named her show *Cooking with Lynja*, and it has several million viewers. Another star is a ninety-three-year-old woman named Lillian Droniak, whose media name is Grandma Droniak, who has 12 million followers on TikTok. A widow and retired factory worker, Lillian has become a senior influencer. She is witty and offers amusing advice about dating and living life to the fullest. She often shoots her own videos with her cell phone. She began doing this because she was bored. In addition to her 12 million fans on TikTok, she also has 1.9 million on Instagram. Her authentic personality and sense of humor resonate with people in several age groups, according to one of her sponsors. Lillian says her work helps her feel less lonely and keeps her busy. She loves the fact that so many followers wish they had a grandma like her. (See Lori Iannou, "Forget Retirement, Become a Social Media Star Instead," *Wall Street Journal*, October 30, 2023, p. R6.)

While some of these entertainers have found fame and fortune in old age, this is not everyone's experience. President Joe Biden, despite a stellar record of political accomplishments, faces a great deal of ageist discrimination in American society today. So, while some change is occurring, prejudices against older Americans remain strong. Indeed, I confront them in myself at times.

Disasters

When we feel as if we've been smashed by life, and we've fallen to pieces, we can take the pieces and with God's help make a new life. Disaster comes in many forms: divorce, illness, accidents, business failure, death of family members or friends, and aging. But we don't have to be defined by our catastrophes. As artists of our own lives, we can transform the broken pieces into a new mosaic of life. Life itself is effective therapy, as psychotherapist Karen Horney suggests.

As I age, I find I often interpret change as a disaster, but I don't have to. Change is just change. It's natural. Inevitable. But it may feel like a disaster sometimes. An example is my newspaper delivery. For years I received the paper at about 5:00 a.m. each morning. I didn't need it this early, but occasionally I read part of it and then returned to sleep. It was always there if I got up at 6:00 or 6:30. After my reliable delivery person quit, for several months I have had the paper arrive at 8:00, 10:00, 11:00, or even later. Initially, I considered this a disaster. Since this change began in the summer of 2022, and it's April 2023 while I am writing this, I am more used to it. I seldom let it ruin my day as

I initially did. Perhaps it's because it has begun arriving more often at 8:00 a.m. Of course, this was not a disaster but a bother. The good news is that at Eastmont my papers come every day at about 4:30 a.m. So this is another positive feature of living here. That and the fact that two other residents now share the cost of the *Wall Street Journal.* That is a boon.

Conclusion

After moving to Eastmont, I have become more familiar with death, dying, and hospice. At a Sunday lunch, the daughter of one of the residents explained that one has choices in hospice care. Her mother had played the accordion, so the daughter chose a music therapist as a hospice helper. This person played the harp for her mother as she languished. I hadn't known there were different sorts of hospice aides. Fortunately, I have also discovered that a friend, an Episcopal priest, Mary Hendricks, also works part-time as a hospice consultant. I hadn't known this until Mary read this manuscript. So, if she is still around when I am dying, I would appreciate her services at my end. She's a very gentle and reassuring person. I'm sure she would talk me through any fears or concerns I might still have about dying.

Of course, we are not all alike. As I served as my brother's night nurse a few years ago, I learned that he had a hospice minister available to him, but he never invited him over to talk. Walt had been in countless nursing homes and hospitals, so he had decided he wanted to die at home with friends around. He didn't seem to want to talk about death, but he had taken care of the details such as paying for his cremation when he would die. He did invite his lawyer to his apartment to make sure all his affairs were in order, and his daytime caregiver knew his wishes. Perhaps he felt prepared because his wife had died several years earlier. For whatever reason, he never spoke to anyone that I knew of, including me, about his fears or hopes about death and the afterlife. He never hushed me when I spoke of the angels watching over us as we returned to sleep after I had given him his morphine at night. He never said anything religious to me. He never engaged in what I considered religious talk. Still, he appreciated the prayers of my prayer group for him on Sundays when we gathered on Zoom. So, he wasn't impervious to religious comfort.

We die in different ways. Some die with the comfort of ministers, friends, and relations around; some in hospitals; some at home. Death comes to us all in different ways, sometimes in the natural order when we are old and worn out, sometimes not. We seem to meet it in our own way. Speaking to a friend the other day, I reassured her that we don't have to be brave when we die. It's OK to be afraid, if we are. God won't mind if we are not brave. We don't have to lay that admonition on ourselves.

Death and Transformation

When I talk to friends about death and heaven, I hear a lot of different ideas. In his book of Devotions, number 17, John Donne spoke of heaven in terms of books. He wrote:

> ... all mankind is of one author, and is one volume; when one man dies, one chapter is not torn out of the book, but translated into a better language; and

Conclusion

every chapter must be so translated; God employs several translators; some pieces are translated by age, some by sickness, some by war, some by justice; but God's hand is in every translation, and his hand shall bind up all our scattered leaves again for that library where every book shall lie open to one another. (John Donne, *Devotions upon Emergent Occasions*, 1960, pp. 108–109.)

In his novel *The Librarian of Saint Malo*, Mario Escobar also writes metaphorically of books and heaven. One of his characters says to another:

I love you too. Please, be happy, and don't forget me. I'll be waiting for you on the other side. I imagine heaven like a huge library, and each of the millions of volumes recounts the life of one of the billions of people who've walked the face of this earth. Nothing will be erased, nothing forgotten.
I held him and let the book slide to the floor. His body eased little by little as his soul ascended to his paradise, the library where each soul held its story until the seals would one day be opened and those souls would be reborn to make a new heaven and a new earth. (Mario Escobar, *The Librarian of Saint Malo*, trans. Thomas Nelson, Nashville, TN: Harper Collins, 2021, p. 179.)

We don't really know what heaven will be like, but Jesus said in his Father's house are many mansions. So there seem to be many possibilities. Some of my friends think we all go to heaven. Some think we go to purgatory first. Some believe in hell as well as heaven. Some think that when we die, that's it. Nothing but darkness. I've been pondering this question off and on for years but especially while writing this book. While my primary purpose has been to write about how to age well and be comforted in our spirits, I have wondered how to approach this topic since I don't have a well-thought-out answer. What occurred to me this morning was imaginative. I've often heard people speak of injured and diseased people being healed of their physical afflictions after they died. I wondered this morning if God improves us before we go to heaven. Maybe in addition to healing our physical bodies, God heals our psychological, spiritual, and even criminal wounds as we are transformed for heaven. Maybe this is what sanctification is. I'm not sure, but I'll keep thinking about it. I realize that if God cares about us enough to create us and sustain us, perhaps God transforms us to be in communion in eternity too. This might take a while. Maybe we linger in what Catholics used to call purgatory. Who knows? All we know is that Jesus died a terrible death by crucifixion yet was transfigured into life anew in the resurrection. And that Jesus offers us eternal life and transformation too.

At a recent funeral, the thought occurred to me that maybe death is like retirement—we know when it is time to retire, so perhaps we will also know when to let go and die. Something to ponder.

Life is uncanny and mysterious as it lives through us. It surprises us!

Conclusion

A closing scripture comes from 1 Corinthians 1:8.

God will strengthen us to the end ...

I am hoping you are pleasantly surprised by life as you read this.

Acknowledgments

Writing a manuscript doesn't make a book.

The writer needs a dedicated editor like Linnea Fredrickson at the University of Nebraska–Lincoln Libraries to smooth out the rough spots and to gracefully alter uneven prose. Linnea does this so well and has done it for three of my previous books. I am so grateful for her and her skillful work.

A book also requires a designer to fashion the book cover to make it appealing to readers. I had no idea how Paul Royster could possibly imagine a cover for this book about aging and spirituality. As usual, he outdid himself in choosing an interesting set of stones precariously balanced with a background of a sunrise or sunset, depending on the viewer's perception. As a helpful publisher, Paul also set the type, provided an ISBN, and arranged for Zea Books in the Digital Commons for publication.

So, many thanks to Linnea and Paul for turning my manuscript into a book.

I also want to thank friends and relations who have encouraged me along the way. You know who you are, and I am grateful.

Finally, thanks to the "Spirit that moves us" for energy, discipline, and inspiration in writing. Thanks also for Scripture, devotions, secular literature, and sacred music, which have strengthened me in this endeavor.

Sincerely,
Marcelline Hutton

www.ingramcontent.com/pod-product-compliance
Lightning Source LLC
Chambersburg PA
CBHW020936090426
42736CB00010B/1161